AI
for
Global Good

Accelerating SDGs in the Age of Innovation

René C Mugenzi

DEDICATION

To my three beloved children
Seeing you grow and dreaming of the world you deserve to live in,
inspires me every day.

It is my deep wish that you, and all of humanity, inherit a future that is
fairer, safer, more compassionate, and sustainable.

This book is a part of that journey. A contribution through research,
information, and reflection, aimed at building the better tomorrow you
deserve.

May this work, and others like it, help shape a world where your
potential and humanity's collective promise can fully flourish.

Table of Contents

ACKNOWLEDGMENTS

This book is the result of a journey shaped by many people, ideas, and moments of reflection. I extend my deepest gratitude to those who walked alongside me on this path.

To my three children and partner your presence in my life gives meaning to everything I do. It is your future that fuels my purpose. May this book serve as a small step toward the better, more just world you and your generation deserve.

To my family and friends, thank you for your constant encouragement, patience, and understanding as I dedicated time and energy to this work.

To my mentors, peers, and collaborators in the fields of technology, development, and public policy your insights, research, and vision have helped shape the framework and content of this book. You continue to inspire me with your commitment to ethical innovation and social transformation.

To those working tirelessly across the globe **to advance the Sustainable Development Goals:** educators, activists, scientists, policymakers, entrepreneurs, and communities you are the true architects of change. This book is for you.

And finally, to every reader engaging with this work thank you for your curiosity, your commitment to a better world, and your belief that the future can, and must, be shaped by our shared values.

With gratitude,

Rene C Mugenzi

AI for Global Good

Chapter 1:
AI's Role in Achieving the Sustainable Development Goals (SDGs)

In 2015, the United Nations adopted the 2030 Agenda for Sustainable Development a blueprint for achieving a better and more sustainable future for all. Central to this agenda are the *17 Sustainable Development Goals (SDGs)*, a set of interconnected objectives designed to tackle some of the most pressing global challenges. These include ending poverty and hunger, ensuring quality education, promoting gender equality, securing access to clean water and affordable energy, fostering inclusive economic growth, and combating climate change. The SDGs recognise that social, economic, and environmental sustainability are interdependent and must be addressed in a unified manner.

Each SDG is underpinned by a series of targets and indicators, which serve as measurable benchmarks for progress. These targets aim to promote inclusivity, equity, resilience, and long-term prosperity for all communities, irrespective of geography or income level. However, as the world approaches the halfway mark toward the 2030 deadline, progress across several goals remains inconsistent. Issues such as climate change, economic inequality, health crises, and geopolitical instability have hampered advancement in many regions.

Achieving the SDGs requires coordinated action across sectors and borders, and increasingly, attention has turned to technology as a catalyst for change. Among emerging technologies, Artificial Intelligence (AI) stands out as a powerful enabler, with the capacity to analyse complex data, automate decision-making, and uncover new insights. Its integration into development efforts could radically accelerate progress across all 17 goals, provided it is deployed ethically and inclusively.

The Transformative Potential of AI

Artificial Intelligence refers to the ability of machines to perform tasks that typically require human intelligence such as learning, reasoning, problem-solving, and perception. With advancements in machine learning, natural language processing, computer vision, and robotics, AI has evolved from a niche field into a transformative force impacting virtually every aspect of society.

When applied to sustainable development, AI can enhance our understanding of global challenges, optimise the delivery of essential services, and drive innovation at scale. It enables governments to make data-informed policy decisions, empowers businesses to adopt sustainable practices, and provides communities with tools to address their specific needs. In this sense, AI is not merely a technological advancement it is a strategic asset in the global pursuit of the SDGs.

1. Data Analysis and Monitoring: AI excels at processing large volumes of data, uncovering patterns, and generating insights. For SDG monitoring, AI can synthesise data from satellites, social media, sensors, and surveys to track indicators in real time. This capability is particularly valuable in areas where traditional data collection is slow, costly, or incomplete. For example, AI can estimate poverty levels by analysing nighttime light emissions from satellite images or predict food insecurity based on weather and crop data.

2. Service Delivery and Optimisation: In healthcare, AI is already being used to diagnose diseases, forecast outbreaks, and optimise resource allocation. In education, adaptive learning platforms personalise content for students based on their learning pace and style. In agriculture, AI systems help farmers monitor soil health, predict yields, and manage pests more effectively. Across sectors, AI reduces inefficiencies, saves costs, and expands reach.

3. Disaster Preparedness and Climate Resilience: AI plays a critical role in environmental sustainability and disaster management. Machine learning models can forecast extreme weather events, monitor deforestation, and detect pollution levels with high accuracy. These tools enable early warning systems and targeted interventions, protecting vulnerable communities and ecosystems.

4. Financial Inclusion and Economic Empowerment: AI-driven platforms are helping unbanked populations access credit and insurance through alternative data analysis. By examining mobile phone usage, transaction patterns, and social connections, AI can create risk profiles for individuals with no formal financial history. This promotes inclusive growth and supports entrepreneurship in underserved regions.

5. Governance and Transparency: AI can improve governance by enhancing transparency, detecting fraud, and streamlining public services. Automated systems reduce bureaucratic delays, while AI-driven analytics help policymakers design evidence-based interventions. Tools such as natural language processing enable the analysis of legislative documents, news reports, and public sentiment to gauge policy impact and public engagement.

Despite these benefits, the transformative power of AI comes with challenges. Bias in algorithms, lack of transparency, and risks of surveillance and automation-led job displacement raise ethical and social concerns. Without inclusive design and equitable access, AI may exacerbate existing inequalities rather than alleviate them. Therefore, harnessing AI for the SDGs requires deliberate efforts to ensure it is inclusive, transparent, accountable, and aligned with human rights.

Purpose and Scope of the Book

This book, **AI for Global Good: Accelerating SDGs in the Age of Innovation,** explores how Artificial Intelligence can serve as a tool for advancing the United Nations Sustainable Development Goals. It seeks to bridge the gap between technological potential and practical implementation, offering insights into the applications, benefits, and risks of AI across each of the 17 SDGs.

The primary aims of this book are to:

Demystify AI: Provide readers with a foundational understanding of what AI is, how it works, and why it matters in the context of sustainable development.

Showcase Impact: Highlight real-world examples of how AI is being used to address social, environmental, and economic challenges—from combating climate change to improving healthcare access.

Encourage Ethical Use: Explore the ethical implications of AI and advocate for responsible, inclusive, and human-centred approaches to its development and deployment.

Promote Collaboration: Emphasise the importance of multi-stakeholder collaboration including governments, businesses, academia, and civil society in designing and scaling AI solutions that align with the SDGs.

Provide Policy Guidance: Offer recommendations on governance, regulation, and capacity-building to ensure that AI supports equitable and sustainable outcomes.

Each chapter of this book focuses on a specific SDG, examining how AI technologies can contribute to its achievement.

Through thematic analysis, case studies, and strategic insights, the chapters aim to answer the following questions:

- What role can AI play in addressing the core challenges of this goal?

- What are the existing AI applications or innovations relevant to the goal?
- What ethical, technical, or societal challenges must be addressed?
- How can policymakers, practitioners, and technologists collaborate effectively?
- What are the opportunities for scale, inclusion, and long-term impact?

Beyond examining individual goals, the book also considers cross-cutting themes such as digital inclusion, AI ethics, data governance, public-private partnerships, and the future of work. These overarching discussions are critical to understanding how AI can be leveraged responsibly and equitably.

Importantly, this book is written for a diverse audience. Policymakers will find actionable recommendations to inform regulation and strategy. Business leaders will discover opportunities for responsible innovation. Technologists will gain insight into the development of inclusive AI systems. Educators and students will access a comprehensive resource for learning and teaching. Civil society actors will better understand how to advocate for transparency and fairness in AI initiatives.

In addition, the book aims to empower readers in developing countries and marginalised communities—

those most often excluded from global tech dialogues—
to engage with AI as a driver of development and
justice. By foregrounding local voices, community-
based innovation, and context-sensitive approaches,
the book strives to ensure that AI for global good truly
includes all.

In sum, **AI for Global Good** is both a guide and a call
to action. It invites readers to reimagine the role of
technology—not as an abstract force or a source of
disruption—but as a partner in building a more just,
equitable, and sustainable world. Through practical
insight and a shared commitment to the SDGs, AI can
become a beacon of possibility in addressing the
defining challenges of our time.

Chapter 2:
The Intersection of AI and Global Challenges

Understanding the Ethical and Social Implications of Artificial Intelligence AI.

Artificial Intelligence (AI) is not just a technological phenomenon—it is a socio-technical system that reflects, amplifies, and potentially reshapes human values and power structures. As AI systems are increasingly integrated into decision-making processes in healthcare, education, policing, finance, and beyond, their social and ethical implications demand serious attention. Understanding these implications is critical to ensuring that AI serves the global good rather than perpetuating existing inequalities or creating new forms of harm.

One of the central ethical concerns in AI development is **bias and discrimination**. AI systems are trained on data historical, social, and often deeply flawed. If that data reflects societal biases, the AI can inherit and even amplify them. For example, facial recognition software has been shown to have higher error rates for individuals with darker skin tones due to underrepresentation in training datasets.

In recruitment, AI algorithms trained on historical hiring patterns may inadvertently penalise women or minority candidates if past decisions were biased. Without active mitigation, these systems risk reinforcing exclusion and marginalisation.

Opacity and accountability also pose significant ethical challenges. Many AI systems, particularly those based on deep learning, operate as 'black boxes', producing outcomes that are difficult to interpret even by their creators. This lack of transparency can make it hard to challenge or contest decisions, especially in high-stakes areas like criminal sentencing or credit approval. If an AI denies someone a loan or places a person under heightened surveillance, who is responsible the developer, the deploying institution, or the machine itself? Without clear lines of accountability, public trust in AI systems erodes.

Another concern lies in the erosion of privacy. AI thrives on data often personal and sensitive. As surveillance technologies become more sophisticated, there is a risk of normalising intrusive data collection in the name of convenience, security, or efficiency. In authoritarian contexts, AI tools such as facial recognition or predictive policing can be used to suppress dissent and monitor citizens in ways that undermine human rights. Even in democratic societies, the line between security and surveillance can be dangerously thin without appropriate safeguards.

Furthermore, AI raises critical questions about **autonomy and human agency.** As machines take over decision-making roles, there is a risk that human judgement becomes secondary or sidelined. In medical diagnostics, for instance, over-reliance on AI tools could discourage second opinions or nuanced assessments. Similarly, in education, adaptive learning systems might inadvertently narrow learning experiences by overly tailoring content to predefined patterns, limiting creativity and critical thinking.

Lastly, the **impact of AI on labour** cannot be ignored. Automation powered by AI threatens to displace workers, particularly in routine or manual jobs. While new opportunities will arise, the transition is unlikely to be evenly distributed, potentially exacerbating unemployment and economic inequality. Workers in low- and middle-income countries, or those in precarious employment, are especially vulnerable if reskilling programmes and social protections are not adequately implemented.

Opportunities and Risks

Despite these concerns, AI also offers unprecedented opportunities to address complex global challenges. Its capacity to process vast datasets, recognise patterns, and automate tasks can enhance decision-making, improve public services, and foster innovation. When deployed responsibly, AI has the potential to serve as a force multiplier for sustainable development.

In **healthcare**, AI enables faster and more accurate diagnoses, predictive modelling of disease outbreaks, and personalised treatment plans. During the COVID-19 pandemic, AI tools were used to track infection rates, forecast hospital demand, and accelerate vaccine research. These innovations save lives and increase the efficiency of overburdened health systems.

In **climate action**, AI contributes to modelling environmental systems, optimising energy consumption, and supporting early warning systems for natural disasters. AI algorithms analyse satellite data to detect deforestation, monitor air quality, and track wildlife populations, aiding conservation efforts. Smart grids use AI to balance energy loads and integrate renewable sources more effectively, reducing carbon emissions.

In **agriculture**, AI supports precision farming—using data on soil conditions, weather patterns, and crop health to inform planting, irrigation, and harvesting decisions. This not only boosts productivity but also reduces the use of water, fertilisers, and pesticides, making farming more sustainable.

In **education**, AI-driven platforms personalise learning, adapt to student needs, and expand access to quality resources. Language translation tools break down barriers for learners in diverse contexts, and AI tutors can provide support where teachers are scarce. These tools have the potential to bridge gaps in access and quality, especially in remote or underserved regions.

However, each of these opportunities comes with corresponding risks. In healthcare, biased algorithms can lead to misdiagnosis or unequal treatment outcomes. In climate action, AI-powered surveillance tools could be misused for control rather than conservation. In agriculture, dependence on AI may marginalise small-scale farmers without access to digital infrastructure. In education, over-reliance on AI could standardise learning in ways that suppress diversity of thought or cultural specificity.

Moreover, the **global AI landscape is uneven**, with high-income countries dominating development and deployment. Without deliberate efforts to democratise access, the benefits of AI risk being concentrated in the hands of a few, while others remain digitally excluded.

This inequality is mirrored in the AI workforce, where gender, racial, and geographic diversity remain limited. A more inclusive AI ecosystem—where communities are not only consumers but also co-creators of technology is essential for global equity.

Building Responsible AI Systems

In order to navigate the opportunities and risks of AI, it is imperative to build systems that are transparent, accountable, inclusive, and aligned with ethical principles. Responsible AI development requires a multi-stakeholder approach, involving governments, academia, civil society, industry, and affected communities.

1. Establishing Ethical Guidelines and Frameworks

Many organisations and governments have developed principles to guide ethical AI, including fairness, accountability, transparency, and human-centred design. However, translating these principles into practice remains a challenge.

Ethical AI requires concrete tools, standards, and regulatory mechanisms that can assess and enforce compliance. This may involve ethical impact assessments, third-party audits, and participatory design processes that involve affected stakeholders in shaping AI systems.

2. Ensuring Inclusivity and Diversity: Responsible AI systems must be inclusive—not only in terms of access but also in terms of design and development. This means diversifying the AI workforce, ensuring representation of different genders, ethnicities, regions, and disciplines. It also means engaging communities in co-creation, recognising that local knowledge and lived experiences are essential to building systems that are contextually appropriate and just.

3. Promoting Transparency and Explainability: To foster trust, AI systems must be transparent about how they function and why they produce specific outcomes. Explainable AI techniques aim to make algorithms more interpretable, providing users with clear rationales behind decisions. This is particularly important in high-stakes contexts, such as criminal justice or healthcare, where opacity can lead to harmful consequences.

4. Safeguarding Data Rights and Privacy: AI must be built on a foundation of data protection and privacy. Robust data governance frameworks should ensure informed consent, data minimisation, and secure storage. Technologies like differential privacy and federated learning can help protect user data while enabling machine learning. Moreover, data collection should be purposeful, proportionate, and respectful of individual and group rights.

5. Encouraging Accountability and Redress Mechanisms: When AI systems cause harm or error, there must be clear pathways for accountability and redress. This includes assigning responsibility to developers, deployers, and institutions. Regulatory bodies may need to establish certification processes or liability standards for AI products. Just as importantly, individuals affected by AI decisions should have the right to appeal or contest those decisions through accessible mechanisms.

6. Bridging the Global Digital Divide: To ensure that AI contributes to inclusive development, efforts must be made to close the digital divide. This includes investing in digital infrastructure, supporting digital literacy, and enabling access to open-source AI tools. International cooperation and technology transfer are crucial in helping low- and middle-income countries participate in and benefit from the AI revolution.

7. Fostering Global Cooperation: Finally, building responsible AI requires global cooperation. AI technologies do not respect national boundaries; their impacts are global and so must be the solutions. Initiatives such as UNESCO's Recommendation on the Ethics of AI, the Global Partnership on AI (GPAI), and various UN agencies are leading efforts to align AI governance with human rights and sustainable development. Continued engagement between nations, supported by a shared commitment to ethical principles, is essential for steering AI in a direction that benefits all.

Finally, intersection of AI and global challenges is both promising and precarious. AI has the potential to unlock transformative solutions to poverty, inequality, health, education, and environmental degradation. Yet, without thoughtful design, inclusive governance, and ethical oversight, it can also entrench injustice and exclusion.

This chapter has laid the groundwork for understanding why AI must be approached not only as a technological tool but as a social force with far-reaching implications. As we move forward in exploring AI's role in achieving the Sustainable Development Goals, the lessons of this chapter should serve as a constant reminder: the future of AI is not predetermined. It will be shaped by the choices we make choices about whose voices we include, whose rights we protect, and whose futures we prioritise.

In this shared endeavour, building responsible AI systems is not just a technical task, it is a moral imperative

Chapter 3:
AI Governance and Ethical Frameworks for Global Good

As *Artificial Intelligence (AI)* continues to evolve and become embedded in our daily lives from healthcare and education to finance, agriculture, and governance the need for strong ethical frameworks and governance mechanisms has become critical.

AI offers immense opportunities for driving social progress, accelerating development, and addressing global challenges. However, without robust governance, the very technologies meant to serve the common good could deepen inequalities, violate rights, and perpetuate systemic harms.

This chapter explores the key dimensions of AI governance, including regulatory challenges, ethical principles such as fairness and accountability, and the need for international cooperation to ensure AI contributes positively to global development.

Regulatory Challenges and Frameworks.

Governance of AI is a complex and evolving field. Traditional regulatory models struggle to keep pace with the speed and scale of AI innovation. Many existing laws and institutions were designed for slower-moving technologies and are ill-equipped to address the nuanced and emergent risks posed by AI systems. This creates a governance gap that must be addressed proactively.

One major challenge is the **lack of standardisation** across jurisdictions. Different countries are at various stages of AI policy development, and approaches vary widely—from permissive environments that encourage innovation to more precautionary frameworks aimed at mitigating risk. This patchwork of regulation can lead to uncertainty for developers and users and may encourage regulatory arbitrage, where companies move operations to less stringent regions.

Additionally, **regulating AI across different sectors** poses unique difficulties. An AI system used in autonomous vehicles faces different risks and expectations than one used in healthcare diagnostics or predictive policing. Sector-specific regulations are essential, but they must be harmonised with overarching ethical principles. Policymakers face the dual challenge of being technology-neutral while also context-sensitive.

Another regulatory hurdle is **ensuring adaptability**. AI systems are not static; they evolve based on data inputs, learning environments, and feedback loops. This means that regulations must be dynamic, allowing for continuous monitoring and iterative updates. Static rules, however well-intentioned, risk becoming obsolete or ineffective.

Furthermore, **enforcement mechanisms** are underdeveloped. Even where AI regulations exist, there is often a lack of institutional capacity to monitor compliance, investigate harms, or hold actors accountable. Strengthening oversight bodies, investing in regulatory expertise, and involving independent audit institutions are necessary steps toward more effective governance.

Fairness, Accountability, and Transparency

A cornerstone of ethical AI governance is the commitment to fairness, accountability, and transparency—often summarised as the FAT principles. These principles aim to ensure that AI technologies do not reinforce discrimination, operate without oversight, or make decisions that are unintelligible to the people they affect.

Fairness in AI refers to both process and outcome. It involves preventing discriminatory practices in algorithm design, training data, and implementation. AI systems trained on biased datasets can perpetuate existing inequalities in areas such as employment, criminal justice, lending, and healthcare. Fairness requires careful scrutiny of data sources, inclusive design teams, and mechanisms to detect and mitigate bias. Importantly, fairness is context-specific—what is fair in one social setting may not be fair in another, necessitating culturally sensitive governance.

Accountability ensures that humans—not algorithms—remain responsible for the consequences of AI decisions. This means identifying who is liable when AI systems fail, produce harm, or violate rights. Accountability frameworks should delineate roles across the AI lifecycle, including developers, data providers, deployers, and decision-makers. Auditable records, risk assessments, and ethical impact evaluations are critical components. Mechanisms for redress and appeal should be built into AI systems, allowing affected individuals to challenge decisions and seek remediation.

Transparency addresses the need for openness in how AI systems work, what data they use, and why they make specific decisions. Transparency builds public trust and enables oversight. This includes explainability, ensuring that AI outcomes can be interpreted and understood by humans, particularly when they affect legal rights or critical services. Transparency also extends to institutional practices: organisations should disclose where and how AI is being used and subject their systems to public scrutiny.

Several emerging tools support the operationalisation of FAT principles. These include algorithmic impact assessments, model cards (documents detailing model performance and limitations), datasheets for datasets, and third-party audits. Embedding these tools into AI development cycles fosters a culture of responsibility and mitigates the risks of opaque and unchecked systems.

International Cooperation for Ethical AI Development

AI is a global phenomenon. Algorithms trained in one part of the world are deployed in another. Data flows across borders. The ethical dilemmas AI presents are not confined to national boundaries. Therefore, international cooperation is essential to ensure that AI development is aligned with shared human values and global priorities, including the Sustainable Development Goals (SDGs).

International cooperation in AI governance can take several forms:

1. Multilateral Agreements and Declarations Global initiatives such as the OECD Principles on AI, the G20 AI Principles, and UNESCO's Recommendation on the Ethics of Artificial Intelligence offer common ground for ethical AI development. These frameworks establish high-level commitments around human rights, sustainability, and inclusivity. While non-binding, they lay the groundwork for more coordinated action and policy harmonisation.

2. International Standards and Benchmarking

Standards bodies such as the *International Organisation for Standardization* (ISO) and the *Institute of Electrical and Electronics Engineers* (IEEE) are developing technical and procedural standards for trustworthy AI.

These standards help align development practices and enable interoperability across jurisdictions. Benchmarking initiatives, where models are evaluated on shared criteria, promote transparency and quality.

3. Global Governance Institutions and Platforms

Efforts are underway to create or expand global institutions dedicated to AI governance. *The Global Partnership on AI (GPAI)*, for instance, brings together governments and experts to conduct collaborative research and policy development.

The UN, through its various agencies, also plays a vital role in facilitating dialogues and coordinating international responses.

4. Capacity Building and Technology Transfer
International cooperation must include support for developing countries to participate in and benefit from AI. This means investing in digital infrastructure, providing training and education, and sharing AI tools and datasets.

Technology transfer, when done equitably, helps reduce global inequalities and fosters innovation ecosystems in underrepresented regions.

5. Cross-border Data Governance AI depends on data, and much of this data is global. Creating fair and secure frameworks for cross-border data sharing is a key challenge. Cooperation is needed to align data protection standards, respect data sovereignty, and prevent misuse. Agreements must strike a balance between enabling innovation and protecting rights.

6. Preventing AI Arms Races and Misuse
International collaboration is also crucial in preventing the militarisation of AI or its use in authoritarian surveillance. Norms, treaties, and monitoring mechanisms should be developed to prohibit harmful applications, such as autonomous weapons or mass surveillance systems that violate privacy and civil liberties.

By fostering international cooperation, the global community can ensure that AI is guided not just by competitive interests but by collective responsibility. Collaboration allows nations to pool knowledge, align ethical standards, and steer innovation toward the common good.

Finally, AI governance and ethical frameworks are essential for ensuring that AI serves as a tool for global good rather than a source of harm or inequality. As AI continues to reshape economies, institutions, and social interactions, our systems of oversight must evolve accordingly. This requires a multifaceted approach strong regulation, ethical principles, inclusive design, and international cooperation.

Fairness, accountability, and transparency must become embedded in the DNA of AI systems. These principles are not mere ideals; they are practical imperatives for trust, legitimacy, and sustainable adoption. Regulators must rise to the challenge of crafting adaptive and sector-specific rules. Developers must embrace tools and practices that prioritise responsibility. Citizens must be empowered to understand, question, and shape the technologies that affect their lives.

Most importantly, nations must work together. The stakes are global and so must be our response. By building governance systems that are anticipatory, inclusive, and collaborative, we can harness AI to advance the Sustainable Development Goals and create a future where technology uplifts rather than undermines human dignity.

Chapter 4:
AI for No Poverty
(SDG 1)

Sustainable Development Goal 1: No Poverty sits at the very heart of the 2030 Agenda for Sustainable Development. It aims to eradicate extreme poverty in all its forms everywhere. Despite significant progress in the early 21st century, the pace of poverty reduction has slowed dramatically, particularly due to the COVID-19 pandemic, ongoing conflicts, and the climate crisis.

Today, hundreds of millions of people continue to live on less than $1.90 a day, with many more vulnerable to falling back into poverty. Addressing poverty requires comprehensive and innovative strategies, and Artificial Intelligence (AI) presents a powerful, albeit underutilised, tool in this endeavour.

AI technologies have the potential to transform how we identify, target, and respond to poverty. By leveraging large datasets and machine learning algorithms, AI can uncover hidden patterns, predict vulnerabilities, and deliver tailored solutions. This chapter explores how AI can contribute to achieving SDG 1 by promoting financial inclusion, supporting effective social protection programmes, and offering scalable insights to policymakers, non-profits, and communities alike.

Using AI for Financial Inclusion and Poverty Reduction

1. Expanding Access to Financial Services

Financial inclusion the availability and equality of opportunities to access financial services is a key driver of poverty reduction.

AI can expand financial inclusion in several ways:

- **Credit Scoring for the Unbanked:** Traditional banking systems rely on credit histories and formal financial records, which many low-income individuals lack. AI offers an alternative by analysing non-traditional data such as mobile phone usage, social media activity, and transaction histories.

  Machine learning models can construct accurate credit profiles for those without bank accounts, enabling access to microloans, insurance, and savings products.

- **Chatbots and Voice Assistants:** AI-powered conversational agents provide financial advice, customer support, and loan information in local languages and dialects.

This lowers the barriers to accessing financial services, especially in rural or illiterate populations. Chatbots also offer 24/7 support, improving service delivery for marginalised users.

- **Fraud Detection and Risk Management**: Financial fraud disproportionately affects vulnerable communities. AI algorithms can detect unusual transaction patterns and flag potential fraud, protecting low-income users and ensuring the integrity of financial systems.

2. Supporting Microenterprises and Informal Workers

Informal economies employ over 60% of the global workforce. These workers often operate without contracts, protections, or access to financial tools.

AI can empower microenterprises by:

- **Market Intelligence**: AI tools analyse market trends, demand fluctuations, and consumer preferences, helping small vendors optimise pricing, manage inventories, and increase profitability.

- **Business Development Services**: AI-driven platforms offer customised business advice, mentorship, and financial literacy training through low-bandwidth mobile apps.

- **Supply Chain Integration:** AI enables small producers to link with broader supply chains by improving logistics, matching supply with demand, and forecasting inventory needs.

3. Enhancing Employment Opportunities

- **Job Matching Platforms:** AI-based employment services match job seekers with suitable opportunities by analysing skill sets, location, experience, and employer needs. These platforms often cater to informal workers, daily wage labourers, and freelancers.

- **Skill Development and E-learning:** AI-powered e-learning platforms provide personalised content to users based on learning pace and career goals. These tools help low-income individuals acquire market-relevant skills and improve their employability.

- **Remote Work Enablement:** AI facilitates remote work for people in poverty-stricken areas by offering real-time translation, transcription, and task automation tools that connect them to global freelance markets.

Predictive Tools for Social Protection Programmes

1. **Targeting and Outreach**
   Accurate identification of beneficiaries is crucial for the success of social protection schemes.

   AI can enhance targeting by:

- **Satellite Imagery and Remote Sensing**: Machine learning applied to satellite data can identify impoverished regions based on housing materials, agricultural patterns, and infrastructure quality.

- **Predictive Poverty Mapping**: AI models integrate diverse data sources—census data, economic indicators, climate data—to create dynamic poverty maps. These maps help governments allocate resources efficiently and ensure aid reaches the most vulnerable.

- **Behavioural Analytics**: AI systems analyse behavioural patterns, such as mobile phone usage and purchasing behaviour, to infer economic vulnerability. This helps reach those who are not captured in formal databases.

2. Programme Design and Adaptation

AI can contribute to designing responsive and adaptive social protection systems:

- **Simulation and Forecasting**: AI models simulate the impact of policy changes, such as cash transfers or subsidies, on different population groups. This supports evidence-based decision-making.

- **Real-Time Needs Assessment**: During crises—such as pandemics, natural disasters, or displacement—AI tools provide real-time insights into emerging needs, allowing for agile programme adjustments.

- **Fraud Detection and Leak Prevention**: AI identifies inconsistencies and anomalies in beneficiary databases and transaction records, reducing fraud and ensuring benefits reach the intended recipients.

3. Monitoring and Evaluation.

Monitoring effectiveness and evaluating impact are essential to the success of social programmes:

- **Impact Measurement**: AI analyses data from surveys, feedback forms, and mobile sensors to assess programme outcomes. This helps identify successful interventions and areas for improvement.

- **Grievance Redress Systems:** Natural language processing enables AI systems to interpret and prioritise citizen complaints, improving responsiveness and accountability.

- **Feedback Loops:** AI enables continuous learning by feeding evaluation data back into programme design, creating adaptive systems that evolve based on performance.

Ethical and Practical Considerations

While the benefits of AI in poverty reduction are significant, they come with important ethical and practical considerations:

- **Bias and Exclusion:** If training data is incomplete or biased, AI models may reinforce existing exclusions. For instance, models based on mobile data may overlook the poorest individuals who lack phone access.

- **Privacy and Consent:** Collecting and analysing personal data must be done with informed consent and strict safeguards. This is especially critical when dealing with vulnerable populations.

- **Digital Divide:** The people most in need of AI-enabled services often face barriers such as lack of connectivity, digital literacy, and appropriate devices. Bridging this divide is essential to ensure inclusive benefits.

- **Transparency and Accountability:** Beneficiaries must understand how decisions are made and have recourse if errors occur. Transparent algorithms and human oversight are necessary.

- **Sustainability:** AI projects should be designed with long-term sustainability in mind, including local capacity building, open-source platforms, and community ownership.

Case Studies and Real-World Applications

1. Kenya's M-Pesa and Credit Scoring: Safaricom's M-Pesa mobile money platform has revolutionised financial inclusion in Kenya. AI-powered credit scoring models analyse transaction histories to offer microloans to users without formal banking history, reducing poverty and boosting entrepreneurship.

2. India's PMGDISHA and AI for Literacy: The Pradhan Mantri Gramin Digital Saksharta Abhiyan (PMGDISHA) aims to improve digital literacy in rural India. AI-driven learning platforms adapt content based on learner progress and feedback, enabling inclusive skill development.

3. Togo's Novissi Programme: During the COVID-19 pandemic, Togo implemented an AI-driven cash transfer programme—Novissi—which used satellite imagery and phone data to identify informal workers affected by lockdowns. This innovative approach enabled rapid, targeted support.

4. World Bank's Poverty Estimation Tools: The World Bank uses AI models to estimate poverty levels in areas with limited survey data. These tools integrate satellite imagery, mobile phone usage, and geospatial data to create real-time poverty maps used for aid allocation.

5. Brazil's Bolsa Família Programme Monitoring: Brazil's conditional cash transfer programme, Bolsa Família, uses AI to monitor compliance, detect anomalies, and evaluate outcomes. AI tools ensure efficient resource use and continuous improvement.

Strategies for Scaling AI for SDG 1

To realise AI's full potential in poverty reduction, a strategic, inclusive, and ethical approach is essential:

1. **Public-Private Partnerships**: Governments, tech companies, and NGOs must collaborate to pool resources, share data, and co-develop AI solutions tailored to local needs.

2. **Open Data and Open-Source Tools**: Open platforms facilitate innovation, transparency, and replication. Sharing models and datasets allows countries and organisations to build on existing solutions.

3. **Digital Infrastructure Investment**: Expanding connectivity, particularly in remote and underserved areas, is critical to enable access to AI-enabled services.

4. **Capacity Building**: Training local stakeholders government officials, community workers, developers is essential to ensure the successful implementation and sustainability of AI projects.

5. **Community Engagement**: Involving local communities in the design, deployment, and evaluation of AI tools ensures that solutions are contextually relevant and culturally sensitive.

6. **Ethical Governance**: Clear frameworks for data governance, algorithmic transparency, and user

protection must be established and enforced to maintain trust and accountability.

AI holds transformative potential for eradicating poverty, but its benefits will not be realised automatically. To make AI work for the world's poorest, we must be intentional, inclusive, and ethical in its design and deployment. From enabling financial inclusion and expanding employment opportunities to optimising social protection systems, AI can offer new pathways out of poverty.

However, these tools must be deployed with a strong emphasis on fairness, privacy, and equity. Technology is not a silver bullet—it is a means to an end.
The ultimate goal must remain the empowerment of individuals and communities to live dignified, self-determined, and prosperous lives. If aligned with human values and guided by inclusive governance, AI can be a powerful ally in the global fight to end poverty in all its forms, everywhere.

Chapter 5:
AI for Zero Hunger
(SDG 2)

Sustainable Development Goal 2: Zero Hunger aims to end hunger, achieve food security, improve nutrition, and promote sustainable agriculture. Despite global commitments, hunger persists and, in some regions, is on the rise. Conflicts, climate change, economic instability, and population growth are contributing to food insecurity worldwide. According to the Food and Agriculture Organization (FAO), over 700 million people globally faced hunger in 2023, a stark reminder of the urgent need for innovation in food systems.

Artificial Intelligence (AI) offers powerful tools to address these challenges. From boosting agricultural productivity to optimising food distribution and reducing waste, AI is transforming how we grow, manage, and consume food.

This chapter explores the potential of AI to advance SDG 2, focusing on its application in precision agriculture, food security, and supply chain efficiency. It also examines the ethical and practical considerations necessary for equitable and sustainable implementation.

AI in Precision Agriculture and Food Security

1. Enhancing Crop Yields and Farm Productivity

Precision agriculture uses AI to make farming more data-driven and efficient. By integrating satellite imagery, sensor data, and weather forecasts, AI systems provide farmers with insights to optimise input use and maximise yields.

- **Soil and Crop Monitoring**: AI-powered sensors monitor soil moisture, nutrient levels, and temperature in real time. This enables precise irrigation and fertilisation, reducing resource waste and improving plant health.

- **Pest and Disease Detection**: Machine learning algorithms analyse images and sensor data to detect early signs of pest infestations or crop diseases. Early intervention minimises crop loss and reduces pesticide use.

- **Yield Forecasting**: AI models predict crop yields based on historical data, weather trends, and remote sensing. These forecasts help farmers and policymakers plan production and distribution more effectively.

2. Supporting Smallholder Farmers

Smallholder farmers produce about 80% of food in developing countries but often lack access to information, technology, and capital.

AI can bridge this gap by:

- **Mobile Advisory Services**: AI-driven platforms provide tailored farming advice via SMS or voice in local languages. These services help farmers make informed decisions on planting, harvesting, and market access.
- **Access to Credit and Insurance**: AI analyses alternative data—such as mobile usage and transaction history to assess creditworthiness, enabling smallholders to access loans and crop insurance.
- **Digital Marketplaces**: AI connects farmers directly with buyers, reducing reliance on intermediaries and improving income. These platforms also predict market trends, guiding pricing strategies.

3. Climate-Resilient Agriculture

Climate change poses a major threat to global food security.

AI supports adaptation through:

- **Climate Forecasting and Risk Modelling**: AI-powered climate models simulate future weather patterns and assess risks to crops and livestock. This helps farmers adapt farming practices and prepare for extreme events.

- **Resilient Crop Breeding**: AI accelerates the development of climate-resilient crop varieties by analysing genetic data and simulating breeding scenarios.

- **Land Use Optimisation**: AI tools evaluate soil types, rainfall, and topography to recommend optimal land use strategies that balance productivity and environmental conservation.

Reducing Food Waste with AI-Driven Supply Chains

1. Optimising Food Distribution

One-third of all food produced globally is wasted much of it due to inefficiencies in the supply chain.

AI improves logistics and storage by:

- **Demand Forecasting**: AI models predict food demand with high accuracy, enabling retailers and suppliers to order and stock more efficiently.

- **Inventory Management**: AI systems track expiration dates, monitor storage conditions, and automate restocking to reduce spoilage.

- **Smart Routing**: AI optimises delivery routes based on traffic, weather, and order volume, ensuring perishable goods reach markets quickly.

2. Reducing Post-Harvest Losses.

In developing regions, post-harvest losses can account for up to 40% of total agricultural output.

AI addresses this issue through:

- **Sensor-Based Monitoring**: IoT devices powered by AI monitor storage facilities for temperature, humidity, and pest activity.

- **Predictive Maintenance**: AI forecasts equipment failure in storage and processing units, preventing breakdowns that lead to spoilage.

- **Grain Quality Assessment:** Computer vision and AI detect contaminants and assess grain quality, ensuring food safety and marketability.

3. Connecting Surplus with Demand

AI facilitates food redistribution by matching surplus with need:

- **Food Recovery Platforms:** AI-powered platforms connect restaurants, supermarkets, and distributors with food banks and charities.

- **Donation Optimisation:** Algorithms recommend optimal times and quantities for donation based on demand forecasts and shelf life.

- **Consumer Behaviour Analysis:** Retailers use AI to analyse purchasing patterns and adjust procurement to minimise overstocking.

Ethical and Practical Considerations

While AI offers significant promise, its application in food systems must be approached responsibly:

- **Data Equity:** Smallholder farmers often generate the data used to train AI systems but may not benefit equitably. Fair data practices and benefit-sharing models are essential.

- **Privacy and Consent:** Data collection must be transparent, with informed consent and strong safeguards, especially when involving personal or sensitive information.

- **Access and Inclusion:** Digital infrastructure gaps can exclude rural and marginalised communities from AI benefits. Investments in connectivity, devices, and digital literacy are critical.

- **Algorithmic Bias:** AI systems trained on data from large-scale farms may not generalise well to smallholder contexts. Inclusive datasets and contextual testing are vital.

- **Environmental Impact:** While AI can reduce waste, its computational demands also consume energy. Sustainable computing practices should be prioritised.

Case Studies and Applications

1. Microsoft AI for Earth and Agrimetrics (UK): Microsoft's AI for Earth programme supports agritech solutions such as Agrimetrics, which uses AI to provide real-time agricultural insights. These tools assist UK farmers in optimising productivity while conserving resources.

2. PlantVillage Nuru (Africa): Developed by Penn State University and the FAO, Nuru is an AI app that helps African farmers detect crop diseases using smartphone images. The app works offline and supports community engagement through farmer-led networks.

3. IBM Watson Decision Platform for Agriculture (Global): This platform integrates weather data, IoT sensors, and AI to support decision-making across the farming value chain. It helps producers manage inputs, reduce waste, and increase output.

4. Wasteless (Israel and Europe) Wasteless is an AI-based pricing solution for retailers that dynamically adjusts prices based on expiry dates. It reduces food waste and increases profit margins.

5. Hello Tractor (Nigeria) Hello Tractor uses AI and IoT to connect smallholder farmers with tractor services. It analyses demand and routes tractors efficiently, improving productivity and reducing manual labour.

Strategies for Scaling AI for Zero Hunger

To maximise the impact of AI in achieving SDG 2, several strategies are recommended:

1. **Public-Private Partnerships:** Collaboration between governments, technology firms, research institutions, and farming communities ensures that AI solutions are relevant, scalable, and sustainable.

2. **Open Access to Agricultural Data:** Sharing anonymised datasets and open-source tools accelerates innovation and fosters transparency.

3. **Capacity Building:** Training farmers, extension workers, and local developers in AI literacy and digital tools ensures meaningful participation.

4. **Community Co-Design:** Involving local communities in designing AI systems ensures cultural relevance and local ownership.

5. **Policy and Regulation:** Clear guidelines on data governance, algorithmic accountability, and environmental standards build trust and guide ethical AI deployment.

6. **Sustainable Financing**: Investments in AI for agriculture must prioritise long-term outcomes, with support for maintenance, updates, and local entrepreneurship.

AI holds transformative potential in the global fight against hunger. By empowering farmers, optimising supply chains, and enabling evidence-based policy, AI can make food systems more productive, resilient, and inclusive.

However, to fulfil this promise, AI must be implemented in ways that prioritise equity, transparency, and sustainability. The path to zero hunger is not only a technological journey but a human one—requiring collaboration, empathy, and a shared commitment to dignity and food for all.

Chapter 6:
AI for Good Health and Well-being
(SDG 3)

Sustainable Development Goal 3: Good Health and Well-being seeks to ensure healthy lives and promote well-being for people of all ages. It encompasses a wide range of targets, including reducing maternal and child mortality, ending epidemics, combating non-communicable diseases, and ensuring universal health coverage.

Despite advancements in medicine and healthcare systems, challenges persist globally. Inequities in access, overburdened facilities, and shortages of skilled health professionals are compounded by emerging threats such as pandemics and climate-related health issues.

Artificial Intelligence (AI) has emerged as a transformative tool with the potential to revolutionise global healthcare. Its ability to process vast datasets, learn from patterns, and provide intelligent decision support makes it particularly suited to improving health outcomes at scale. From enhancing diagnostic accuracy to enabling proactive disease prevention, AI can strengthen health systems, improve equity, and accelerate progress toward achieving SDG 3.

This chapter explores the role of AI in advancing good health and well-being, focusing on AI-powered healthcare diagnostics and predictive analytics for disease prevention.

It also addresses ethical, and implementation challenges and proposes strategies to ensure inclusive and equitable use of AI in health.

AI-Powered Healthcare Diagnostics

1. Enhancing Diagnostic Accuracy and Speed

AI technologies are being applied across a broad spectrum of diagnostic functions, significantly improving the accuracy and efficiency of disease detection.

- **Medical Imaging**: AI algorithms, particularly deep learning models, analyse radiological images—such as X-rays, MRIs, and CT scans—with precision often comparable to, or exceeding, that of human specialists. These tools help detect conditions like cancer, pneumonia, and fractures early, reducing diagnostic errors.

- **Pathology and Histology**: AI systems assist in the analysis of biopsy samples, identifying abnormalities such as tumours or inflammatory markers. Computer vision allows high-throughput screening, increasing diagnostic capacity in resource-constrained settings.

- **Ophthalmology:** AI is used to detect diabetic retinopathy and other eye conditions through retinal scans. This is particularly useful in rural areas where ophthalmologists are scarce.

- **Dermatology:** AI apps analyse images of skin lesions to assess the likelihood of skin cancer, enabling early referrals and reducing unnecessary clinic visits.

- **Cardiology:** AI-powered electrocardiogram (ECG) analysis detects arrhythmias and predicts heart failure with high accuracy, supporting timely interventions.

2. Expanding Access to Diagnostics

In many low- and middle-income countries, access to specialist diagnostics is limited.

AI helps bridge this gap through:

- **Telemedicine Platforms:** AI-integrated telehealth systems offer remote consultations and diagnostic support, improving access in remote areas.

- **Portable Diagnostic Devices:** AI-enhanced point-of-care devices bring diagnostic capabilities to the patient's bedside or community clinic, reducing the need for hospital referrals.

- **AI Chatbots:** Conversational AI tools perform preliminary symptom assessments and triage, guiding patients toward appropriate care.

- **Language and Translation Tools:** Natural language processing enables multilingual diagnostics, breaking down linguistic barriers in healthcare delivery.

3. Workflow Optimisation and Clinical Decision Support

AI streamlines clinical workflows, improving efficiency and reducing the burden on health professionals.

- **Triage and Prioritisation:** AI systems help prioritise cases based on urgency, allowing clinicians to focus on high-risk patients.

- **Electronic Health Records (EHRs):** AI improves the utility of EHRs by summarising patient histories, flagging risks, and recommending actions.

- **Prescription and Treatment Recommendations:** AI tools support clinical decision-making by comparing symptoms, lab results, and treatment protocols.

Predictive Analytics for Disease Prevention

1. Public Health Surveillance and Early Warning

AI is revolutionising disease surveillance and public health intelligence:

- **Outbreak Prediction:** AI models analyse epidemiological, environmental, and mobility data to predict disease outbreaks. For example, AI helped identify early signs of COVID-19 by tracking unusual case patterns and media reports.

- **Zoonotic Disease Monitoring:** AI tracks disease spillover from animals to humans using biodiversity data, helping prevent pandemics.

- **Wastewater Analysis:** AI assists in analysing wastewater data to detect community-level outbreaks of viruses and bacteria.

2. Personalised Prevention and Risk Stratification

AI enables personalised approaches to health promotion and disease prevention:

- **Risk Scoring:** Machine learning models predict individual risk for chronic conditions such as diabetes, hypertension, and cancer based on lifestyle, genetics, and medical history.

- **Behavioural Analytics**: AI analyses wearable data such as activity levels, heart rate, and sleep to identify unhealthy patterns and suggest behaviour modifications.

- **Mental Health Monitoring**: AI-driven platforms assess speech, text, and facial expressions to detect signs of depression, anxiety, or stress, prompting early support.

3. Health System Strengthening

AI strengthens public health infrastructure and planning:

- **Resource Allocation**: Predictive models inform the distribution of vaccines, staff, and medical supplies based on need projections.

- **Screening Programmes**: AI identifies populations at risk and supports large-scale screening campaigns for infectious and non-communicable diseases.

- **Chronic Disease Management**: AI platforms support continuous monitoring and coaching for patients with long-term conditions, reducing hospital visits.

Ethical and Practical Considerations

While AI offers transformative benefits in healthcare, it also raises significant ethical and practical challenges:

- **Bias and Fairness**: AI systems trained on non-representative datasets may underperform for certain populations, reinforcing health disparities.

- **Data Privacy and Consent**: Protecting sensitive health information is critical. AI models must operate within strong data protection frameworks, with informed consent from users.

- **Explainability and Trust**: Black-box algorithms hinder clinical accountability. Explainable AI (XAI) techniques help ensure decisions are transparent and interpretable.

- **Regulatory Compliance**: AI applications in healthcare must meet stringent safety and efficacy standards. Regulatory bodies must develop agile frameworks to evaluate AI tools.

- **Digital Divide**: The benefits of AI may not reach those without internet access, smartphones, or digital literacy. Inclusive design and outreach are essential.

Case Studies and Applications

1. Google DeepMind and Moorfields Eye Hospital (UK): DeepMind developed an AI model capable of diagnosing over 50 eye conditions from retinal scans. The system matches expert performance and is being tested for deployment in NHS clinics.

2. Babylon Health (Global): Babylon Health offers AI-powered virtual consultations and triage tools. Used in Rwanda and the UK, it provides affordable healthcare access through mobile platforms.

3. AI4COVID-19 (Thailand): Thai researchers developed an AI tool to detect COVID-19 from cough sounds. The system provides rapid, contactless screening for use in community settings.

4. BlueDot (Canada): BlueDot's AI system monitors news reports, airline data, and disease alerts to detect outbreaks. It issued an early warning on COVID-19 days before official announcements.

5. Apollo Hospitals' Predictive Analytics (India): Apollo uses AI to predict heart disease risks based on EHRs and lifestyle data. This enables proactive interventions and lifestyle counselling.

Strategies for Scaling AI for SDG 3

To maximise AI's contribution to global health, coordinated efforts are required:

1. **Policy Development:** Governments should establish AI health strategies aligned with national priorities, supported by ethical and legal safeguards.

2. **Capacity Building:** Training programmes for clinicians, data scientists, and regulators are essential to build AI literacy and trust.

3. **Infrastructure Investment:** Expanding digital infrastructure and health data systems enables equitable access to AI-enabled care.

4. **Inclusive Design:** AI tools should be developed with input from diverse communities to ensure relevance and avoid bias.

5. **International Collaboration:** Cross-border data sharing and research partnerships enhance global preparedness and innovation.

6. **Monitoring and Evaluation:** Continuous impact assessment and user feedback loops ensure AI tools remain effective and trustworthy.

Finally, AI represents a paradigm shift in healthcare delivery and public health strategy. From improving diagnostic accuracy to enabling personalised prevention, AI can help realise the vision of SDG 3: ensuring healthy lives and promoting well-being for all.

However, its success hinges on inclusive deployment, ethical governance, and sustained collaboration across sectors and borders.

Technology must serve people—not replace them. With the right guardrails, AI can be a powerful ally in creating health systems that are more responsive, equitable, and resilient.

Chapter 7:
AI for Quality Education
(SDG 4)

Sustainable Development Goal 4: Quality Education aims to ensure inclusive and equitable education and promote lifelong learning opportunities for all. Education is one of the most powerful instruments for reducing poverty, promoting gender equality, and fostering sustainable development. Yet, despite significant strides in expanding access to education globally, millions of children and adults remain excluded, particularly in conflict-affected, rural, and low-income areas.

Inequality in learning outcomes, lack of infrastructure, insufficient teaching resources, and limited support for learners with disabilities continue to hinder progress.

Artificial Intelligence (AI) is poised to transform the global education landscape. Through intelligent systems capable of adapting to individual learners' needs, analysing data at scale, and delivering education across borders and languages, AI offers novel solutions to longstanding educational challenges.

Personalised Learning Systems

1. Adapting to Learners' Needs

AI enables a shift from one-size-fits-all education models to personalised, learner-centred approaches:

- **Adaptive Learning Platforms**: AI-powered systems such as Squirrel AI and Century Tech adjust content difficulty and pace based on learners' responses and progress. These platforms assess learners' strengths and weaknesses in real time and offer targeted feedback.

- **Customised Learning Pathways**: AI algorithms curate tailored curricula and recommend resources aligned with learners' goals, aptitudes, and interests. This ensures deeper engagement and mastery.

- **Learning Style Recognition**: AI identifies whether learners respond better to visual, auditory, or kinesthetic content and modifies teaching methods accordingly.

- **Automated Tutoring and Feedback**: AI tutors provide instant explanations, quizzes, and error corrections, mimicking the support of a human tutor and freeing up educators to focus on higher-order teaching tasks.

2. Supporting Teachers and Institutions

AI complements teachers by offering administrative, analytical, and instructional support:

- **Assessment and Grading**: AI automates grading of multiple-choice questions, short answers, and increasingly, essays. This reduces teachers' workloads and ensures faster feedback for students.

- **Classroom Analytics**: AI analyses attendance, engagement, and performance data to help teachers identify struggling students and tailor interventions.

- **Content Creation**: Natural language generation tools create lesson plans, quizzes, and even reading materials tailored to different skill levels and curricula.

- **Professional Development**: AI platforms recommend training modules for teachers based on classroom data, improving pedagogy and classroom management.

3. Encouraging Self-Directed Learning

Personalised AI tools encourage learners to take ownership of their learning journeys:

- **Gamification and Motivation:** AI tracks progress and awards badges, points, and certifications, motivating learners through game-like elements.

- **Learning Companions:** Virtual assistants engage learners in dialogue, answer questions, and provide encouragement, reducing isolation in online learning environments.

- **Feedback Loops:** AI collects data on learners' responses and adapts instruction dynamically, ensuring continuous alignment with learners' needs and fostering confidence.

Expanding Educational Access in Underserved Regions

1. Overcoming Infrastructure Barriers

AI facilitates educational access where schools and teachers are scarce:

- **Offline AI Platforms:** Tools like Kolibri and Eneza Education offer AI-powered learning resources accessible offline, enabling learning in areas with limited or no internet.

- **Low-Bandwidth Solutions:** AI chatbots and SMS-based tutoring provide support via basic mobile phones, bridging digital divides.

- **Remote Teaching and Learning**: AI supports remote instruction through content curation, lesson delivery, and student assessment, enabling continuity during school closures or crises.

2. Bridging Language and Cultural Gaps

Language and cultural barriers often prevent learners from fully engaging with content:

- **Automated Translation and Transcription**: AI-powered tools like Google Translate and DeepL provide real-time translations, allowing students to access resources in multiple languages.

- **Voice Recognition for Local Dialects**: AI voice assistants trained in indigenous languages help learners access instruction in their mother tongue.

- **Culturally Relevant Content**: AI curates localised educational materials, ensuring relevance and resonance with learners' cultural backgrounds.

3. Supporting Learners with Disabilities

AI enhances inclusivity by accommodating diverse learning needs:

- **Text-to-Speech and Speech-to-Text Tools**: These technologies enable visually impaired and dyslexic learners to access and produce content.

- **AI-Powered Captioning and Sign Language Recognition**: Real-time captioning and sign language interpretation tools help learners with hearing impairments.

- **Cognitive Support Tools**: AI assists learners with autism, ADHD, and other cognitive conditions by adapting content delivery and monitoring stress indicators.

Ethical and Practical Considerations

Deploying AI in education requires careful attention to ethical and logistical factors:

- **Data Privacy**: Student data must be collected, stored, and used ethically. Consent, transparency, and compliance with data protection laws are essential.

- **Algorithmic Fairness**: AI systems must not reinforce existing biases. Models should be tested across diverse demographics to ensure equitable performance.

- **Digital Divide:** Efforts must address disparities in access to devices, connectivity, and digital literacy to avoid widening educational inequality.

- **Teacher Empowerment:** AI should augment, not replace, teachers. Professional development and participatory design ensure teachers remain central to education.

- **Sustainability and Cost:** AI tools must be scalable, maintainable, and financially accessible, especially for low-resource settings.

Case Studies and Applications

1. Squirrel AI (China) This adaptive learning platform uses AI to tailor instruction to individual students in maths and science. Studies show significant improvements in learning outcomes.

2. M-Shule (Kenya) M-Shule uses SMS and AI to deliver personalised learning and analytics to primary school students in Kenya, reaching learners with limited internet access.

3. Content Technologies Inc. (USA) This company uses AI to create customised textbooks and learning materials, adapting content to students' performance and preferences.

4. IBM Watson Education IBM's AI tools support teachers with curriculum planning, student insights, and learning support. Pilot programmes show increased engagement and academic achievement.

5. Talk to Books and Read Along by Google These AI-based tools offer interactive reading experiences, helping children improve language and literacy skills through engaging, conversational learning.

Strategies for Scaling AI for SDG 4

To maximise AI's contribution to education, coordinated action is needed:

1. **Inclusive Policy Development:** Governments should develop AI-in-education strategies that prioritise equity, ethics, and human rights.

2. **Public-Private Partnerships:** Collaboration between ministries, edtech companies, and NGOs ensures innovation aligns with educational goals.

3. **Investing in Infrastructure:** Expanding electricity, connectivity, and device access is foundational for digital learning.

4. **Open Educational Resources (OER):** Supporting open-source, AI-enabled content platforms fosters accessibility and local adaptation.

5. **Capacity Building:** Training educators, administrators, and learners in digital skills ensures effective and ethical use of AI tools.

6. **Monitoring and Evaluation:** Continuous assessment of AI's impact on learning outcomes, equity, and well-being is essential for refinement and accountability.

AI holds the potential to revolutionise education by personalising learning, expanding access, and supporting inclusive pedagogies. Its intelligent adaptability, capacity for data-driven insights, and ability to transcend physical and linguistic barriers make it a critical tool in achieving SDG 4. However, to realise this promise, AI must be developed and deployed ethically, inclusively, and sustainably.

AI should be viewed not as a replacement for teachers but as a companion to human instruction—amplifying what works, innovating where needed, and ensuring no learner is left behind. By embedding equity, transparency, and human dignity into AI-driven education systems, we can build a world where quality learning is a right enjoyed by all.

Chapter 8:
AI for Gender Equality
(SDG 5)

Sustainable Development Goal 5: Gender Equality seeks to achieve equality between women and men and empower all women and girls. Despite global efforts, gender disparities persist across political, economic, educational, and technological domains. Structural inequalities, societal norms, discriminatory laws, and limited access to resources and opportunities continue to disadvantage women and girls worldwide.

Artificial Intelligence (AI), when designed and deployed inclusively, can support the dismantling of these inequalities. It offers new tools for exposing gender-based discrimination, expanding opportunities, amplifying women's voices, and addressing gaps in representation.

However, AI also risks entrenching bias if not carefully managed. This chapter explores the dual role of AI in both challenging and perpetuating gender inequalities. It focuses on strategies for addressing algorithmic bias, promoting women's participation in AI development, and leveraging AI-driven platforms to empower women and girls across sectors.

Addressing Biases and Promoting Women's Participation

1. Recognising and Correcting Gender Bias in AI

AI systems are trained on historical data, which often reflect systemic gender biases. If uncorrected, these biases are encoded into algorithms, producing discriminatory outcomes:

- **Gendered Language and Stereotyping**: Natural language processing tools have replicated and amplified gender stereotypes in text generation, translation, and summarisation tasks.

- **Facial Recognition Disparities**: Studies have shown higher error rates in facial recognition for women, particularly women of colour, due to underrepresentation in training datasets.

- **Hiring Algorithms**: AI recruitment tools have discriminated against female candidates by penalising CVs containing indicators of gender, such as women's colleges or maternity leave.

To mitigate these harms, developers must:

- **Audit Datasets**: Identify and correct gender imbalances and stereotypical representations.

- **Debias Algorithms:** Apply fairness-aware machine learning techniques that adjust outputs to reduce disparate impacts.

- **Evaluate Outcomes:** Conduct gender impact assessments and algorithmic audits throughout the AI lifecycle.

2. Promoting Diversity in AI Development

Inclusive AI systems require diverse design teams that reflect the populations they serve. However, women are significantly underrepresented in AI-related roles:

- Women account for less than 25% of AI professionals globally.

- Leadership roles in AI companies and research institutions remain predominantly male.

Promoting gender diversity in AI development involves:

- **Education and Mentorship:** Initiatives like AI4All and Women in AI provide training and support networks for young women entering the field.

- **Policy and Organisational Change**: Institutions must adopt gender equity policies, track diversity metrics, and foster inclusive cultures.

- **Funding Women-Led Innovation**: Increasing access to capital for women entrepreneurs in AI and supporting women-led research projects.

3. Embedding Gender Perspectives in Design

Gender-inclusive AI design integrates women's perspectives and lived experiences:

- **Participatory Design Methods**: Engaging women users in co-creating AI tools to ensure relevance, usability, and inclusivity.

- **Contextual Sensitivity**: Recognising the intersection of gender with race, class, age, disability, and geography to avoid one-size-fits-all solutions.

- **Inclusive User Testing**: Ensuring that AI systems are evaluated with diverse populations to capture differences in access, behaviour, and impact.

AI-Driven Platforms for Empowering Women and Girls

1. Expanding Educational and Economic Opportunities

AI tools can democratise access to information, skills, and markets for women and girls:

- **Personalised Learning Platforms**: AI-powered e-learning apps tailor content to individual learning styles and life contexts, enabling women and girls to acquire skills at their own pace.

- **Career Counselling and Job Matching**: AI-driven platforms recommend career paths, job opportunities, and online training based on skills and interests.

- **Entrepreneurial Support**: AI chatbots and virtual assistants provide women entrepreneurs with business advice, market intelligence, and legal information.

2. Supporting Health and Well-being

AI technologies support women's health, particularly in areas with limited access to care:

- **Maternal Health Monitoring**: AI-powered mobile tools offer prenatal advice, appointment reminders, and symptom checks for expecting mothers.

- **Reproductive Health Education**: Chatbots provide accurate, confidential information on contraception, menstruation, and sexual health.

- **Gender-Based Violence (GBV) Detection**: AI algorithms identify patterns of abuse in social media, messaging, or hotline transcripts, enabling faster responses from support services.

3. **Enhancing Civic Participation and Advocacy**
AI tools help women engage in public life and amplify their voices:

- **Civic Tech Platforms**: AI supports platforms where women can report public service issues, contribute to policy dialogues, and access legal aid.

- **Sentiment Analysis and Opinion Mining**: These tools track public sentiment on gender issues, helping advocates tailor campaigns and measure impact.

- **Voice Cloning and Accessibility Tools**: AI enables women with disabilities or in remote areas to participate in decision-making forums through translated, subtitled, or voice-enabled platforms.

Ethical and Practical Considerations

The use of AI for gender equality must navigate several challenges:

- **Surveillance and Misuse:** AI tools can be used to monitor and control women, particularly in patriarchal or authoritarian settings.

- **Data Privacy:** Women's data—especially related to health and safety—requires stringent protection against misuse or exposure.

- **Digital Exclusion:** Structural barriers such as lack of internet access, device ownership, or digital literacy disproportionately affect women.

- **Trust and Safety:** Women are more likely to face online harassment. AI platforms must implement robust safety features and moderation protocols.

- **Cultural Context:** Gender norms vary widely. AI tools must be locally adaptable and designed with cultural sensitivity.

Case Studies and Applications

1. SheCodes (Global): This AI-based coding bootcamp tailors training for women and girls, using personalised learning paths and mentorship to address gender gaps in tech.

2. SafeCity (India): SafeCity uses AI to analyse crowdsourced reports of sexual harassment. Data visualisation maps identify hotspots, helping authorities improve safety measures.

3. Viamo's 3-2-1 Service (Sub-Saharan Africa): This AI-powered mobile platform delivers free voice-based education to women in rural areas on topics such as health, farming, and financial literacy.

4. UN Women's Chatbots for GBV Awareness (Global): UN Women has launched AI chatbots to educate users about gender-based violence, rights, and services available. The bots support multiple languages and low-bandwidth environments.

5. Women@AI (Europe and Global South) This initiative supports women researchers and practitioners through networking, funding, and research collaborations aimed at responsible AI development.

Strategies for Scaling AI for Gender Equality

1. **Gender-Inclusive Policy Frameworks:** Governments must integrate gender analysis into national AI strategies and ensure representation in policymaking bodies.

2. **Digital Infrastructure and Literacy:** Investments in broadband, affordable devices, and training programmes are essential for bridging the gender digital divide.

3. **Ethical Standards and Accountability:** Regulations should mandate gender audits, explainability, and redress mechanisms for AI systems that impact women.

4. **Support for Women Technologists:** Scholarships, accelerator programmes, and mentorship should target women entering STEM and AI careers.

5. **Partnerships with Women's Organisations:** Collaborating with grassroots groups ensures AI tools are responsive to the real needs and priorities of women and girls.

6. **Monitoring and Research:** Disaggregated data collection and gender-focused impact studies help assess the effectiveness of AI interventions.

AI has the potential to act as a powerful equaliser by challenging systemic biases, expanding opportunities, and amplifying the voices of women and girls.

However, realising this potential requires deliberate action ensuring that AI systems are not only free from bias but actively designed to promote equity. It also demands the inclusion of women at every stage of AI development, from design and data collection to deployment and governance.

Gender equality is not a side issue—it is central to inclusive and sustainable development. As we harness AI to achieve SDG 5, we must centre dignity, representation, and justice. Only then can AI become a true tool of liberation and empowerment for women and girls everywhere.

Chapter 9:
AI for Clean Water and Sanitation
(SDG 6)

Sustainable Development Goal 6: Clean Water and Sanitation aims to ensure availability and sustainable management of water and sanitation for all. Water is essential for health, food security, biodiversity, and socio-economic development. Yet, billions of people around the world lack access to safely managed drinking water, basic sanitation, and hygiene services. Climate change, population growth, urbanisation, and industrial pollution exacerbate these challenges, placing enormous stress on freshwater resources and infrastructure.

Artificial Intelligence (AI) offers a promising solution to the global water and sanitation crisis. By enabling data-driven decisions, optimising resource allocation, and detecting inefficiencies and risks, AI is revolutionising how water systems are managed and monitored.

Smart Water Management Systems

1. Real-Time Monitoring and Data Integration

AI systems enhance water management by enabling real-time data analysis and actionable insights:

- **Sensor Networks**: AI-powered Internet of Things (IoT) sensors monitor water levels, flow rates, pressure, and quality across rivers, reservoirs, and distribution systems.

- **Data Fusion**: Machine learning integrates diverse data sources—weather forecasts, satellite imagery, historical usage—to provide a comprehensive view of water systems.

- **Anomaly Detection**: AI detects irregularities such as leaks, unauthorised usage, and contamination, triggering alerts for immediate response.

These capabilities improve operational efficiency, reduce waste, and ensure safe and equitable distribution of water.

2. Demand Forecasting and Resource Allocation

Accurate forecasting supports efficient water use:

- **Consumption Modelling**: AI models predict household, agricultural, and industrial water demand based on behavioural patterns and climatic conditions.

- **Irrigation Management**: AI optimises irrigation schedules by analysing soil moisture, crop type, and weather data, reducing water use in agriculture.

- **Water Supply Planning**: Predictive analytics support urban planners in designing resilient water systems by simulating scenarios of demand growth and climate variability.

These tools help utilities balance supply and demand, avoid shortages, and reduce environmental stress.

3. Water Quality Monitoring and Pollution Control

Maintaining water quality is critical for public health and environmental sustainability:

- **Contaminant Detection**: AI analyses chemical, physical, and biological indicators from water samples to identify pollutants.

- **Early Warning Systems:** Real-time AI models flag risks such as algal blooms, chemical spills, or sewage overflows.

- **Remote Sensing:** AI interprets satellite data to monitor water bodies for sedimentation, eutrophication, and illegal dumping.

These capabilities enable preventive interventions and compliance with environmental regulations.

Predictive Tools for Sanitation Infrastructure

1. **Infrastructure Planning and Optimisation**
   Sanitation infrastructure often suffers from underinvestment and poor planning.

   AI can improve design and maintenance:

- **Asset Mapping and Risk Assessment:** AI identifies locations lacking sanitation facilities and prioritises investments based on health risk and population density.

- **Predictive Maintenance:** AI forecasts when pumps, pipes, or treatment plants are likely to fail, enabling preventive repairs.

- **Simulation Tools**: AI-based digital twins simulate wastewater flow and treatment processes, guiding infrastructure upgrades.

This results in more resilient, cost-effective, and inclusive sanitation systems.

2. Wastewater Treatment and Recycling

AI enhances efficiency and sustainability in wastewater management:

- **Process Optimisation**: AI adjusts treatment parameters—such as aeration, pH, and chemical dosing—in real time for optimal performance.

- **Energy Efficiency**: AI minimises energy consumption in treatment plants by balancing load and demand.

- **Water Reuse Monitoring**: AI tracks water quality to ensure recycled water meets safety standards for agricultural or industrial reuse.

These innovations reduce operational costs, conserve water, and lower environmental footprints.

3. Hygiene and Public Health Interventions

AI supports the promotion of hygiene and disease prevention:

- **Disease Surveillance:** AI analyses wastewater for early signs of disease outbreaks, such as COVID-19 or cholera, enabling timely responses.

- **Behavioural Analytics:** Mobile platforms track hygiene behaviour and tailor interventions—such as handwashing campaigns—based on community data.

- **Infrastructure Usage Tracking:** AI monitors usage patterns in public toilets and hygiene stations to improve maintenance and design.

These tools strengthen public health systems and contribute to community well-being.

Ethical and Practical Considerations

Using AI in water and sanitation systems requires consideration of several challenges:

- **Data Quality and Access:** In many regions, reliable data is scarce. Investments in infrastructure and open data policies are necessary.

- **Equity and Inclusion:** AI systems must prioritise marginalised communities that are often excluded from formal water services.

- **Privacy and Consent:** Data collection on water use or sanitation habits must respect user privacy and comply with legal standards.

- **Affordability and Sustainability:** AI solutions should be financially accessible and designed for long-term sustainability, especially in low-resource settings.

- **Human Oversight:** Decisions affecting public health and resource allocation should involve human accountability and community participation.

Case Studies and Applications

1. IBM's Green Horizons (China) IBM's AI platform monitors air and water pollution in Chinese cities. It predicts contamination events and supports environmental planning.

2. CityTaps (Niger) This start-up provides smart water meters powered by AI and IoT, allowing households in low-income urban areas to prepay for water services and manage usage.

3. Aquasight (USA) Aquasight's AI platform helps municipalities monitor drinking water quality, detect leaks, and optimise treatment plant operations.

4. DeepMind and Thames Water (UK) DeepMind is working with Thames Water to predict sewer blockages using AI, reducing overflows and environmental damage.

5. Sanergy (Kenya) Sanergy uses AI to optimise collection routes for its container-based sanitation service in informal settlements, improving reliability and coverage.

Strategies for Scaling AI for SDG 6

To harness AI effectively for clean water and sanitation, the following strategies are essential:

1. **Policy Integration:** Governments should integrate AI into national water and sanitation strategies, backed by ethical guidelines and standards.

2. **Infrastructure Investment:** Expanding digital and physical infrastructure is key to deploying AI tools in underserved regions.

3. **Capacity Building**: Training for engineers, policymakers, and utility workers on AI literacy and operations ensures sustainable implementation.

4. **Open Data Initiatives**: Encouraging data sharing among governments, researchers, and NGOs fosters innovation and accountability.

5. **Community Engagement**: Involving communities in the design and monitoring of AI-enabled systems builds trust and local relevance.

6. **Cross-Sector Collaboration**: Partnerships between technology firms, water utilities, academic institutions, and civil society accelerate development and scaling.

AI can play a critical role in ensuring clean water and sanitation for all. Through intelligent monitoring, predictive maintenance, and data-driven planning, AI supports more efficient, resilient, and inclusive water and sanitation systems.

However, success depends on ensuring that AI solutions are equitable, ethical, and accessible especially for the communities most in need.

By aligning technological innovation with human rights and environmental sustainability, AI can help transform the water and sanitation landscape and accelerate progress toward SDG 6.

Chapter 10:
AI for Affordable and Clean Energy
(SDG 7)

Sustainable Development Goal 7: Affordable and Clean Energy aims to ensure access to affordable, reliable, sustainable, and modern energy for all. Energy is a cornerstone of development, influencing health, education, economic growth, and environmental sustainability. Yet more than 750 million people worldwide still live without electricity, and many more rely on polluting and inefficient energy sources. As the global population grows and demand for energy intensifies, there is an urgent need to transition to renewable energy sources and improve energy efficiency.

Artificial Intelligence (AI) is emerging as a transformative force in the energy sector. With its ability to process vast amounts of data, predict trends, and optimise systems in real time, AI enables smarter generation, distribution, and consumption of energy.

Optimising Renewable Energy Systems

1. Forecasting and Integration of Renewable Sources

Renewable energy sources such as solar and wind are variable by nature, making accurate forecasting essential for reliable grid operation.

AI supports this by:

- **Weather Forecasting**: Machine learning models analyse meteorological data to predict solar irradiance, wind speeds, and cloud cover, improving generation forecasts.

- **Energy Yield Prediction**: AI estimates energy output from solar panels or wind turbines based on real-time and historical data.

- **Grid Balancing**: AI integrates forecasts with demand data to match supply and demand, reducing curtailment and increasing renewable penetration.

These tools enable grid operators to plan ahead, minimise reliance on fossil fuels, and maintain energy reliability.

2. System Design and Performance Optimisation

AI contributes to more efficient renewable energy systems through:

- **Turbine and Panel Placement:** AI analyses terrain, wind flow, and sunlight patterns to optimise the placement of turbines and panels for maximum efficiency.

- **Operational Efficiency:** AI monitors energy systems and adjusts parameters to maximise performance. For example, AI can change the tilt of solar panels or pitch of turbine blades in response to environmental conditions.

- **Maintenance Prediction:** AI-powered predictive maintenance identifies potential faults before they lead to failure, reducing downtime and maintenance costs.

By enhancing performance and reducing costs, AI accelerates the viability and adoption of renewable energy technologies.

3. Scaling Access in Remote and Off-Grid Areas

AI facilitates decentralised energy solutions:

- **Microgrid Management:** AI optimises microgrids— small-scale local energy networks—by predicting usage patterns and balancing generation, storage, and demand.

- **Site Selection and Demand Estimation**: AI identifies optimal locations for off-grid renewable systems by analysing population density, energy needs, and infrastructure gaps.

- **Remote Monitoring**: AI enables real-time monitoring of remote energy systems, improving reliability and reducing maintenance costs.

These applications expand energy access to underserved populations, promoting equity and resilience.

AI-Powered Energy Storage and Distribution

1. Smart Energy Storage Systems

Effective energy storage is vital for balancing supply and demand in renewable energy systems. AI enhances storage through:

- **Battery Management**: AI predicts battery charge/discharge cycles, prolonging battery life and ensuring efficient use.

- **Optimising Energy Flows**: AI determines when to store or release energy based on grid conditions and price signals.

- **Hybrid Systems**: AI coordinates between multiple storage types (e.g., batteries, pumped hydro, thermal storage) for cost-effective energy management.

This improves energy reliability, particularly when renewables are not generating power.

2. Smart Grids and Load Management

AI is central to the development of intelligent, responsive energy grids:

- **Load Forecasting**: AI predicts electricity demand based on time of day, weather, and user behaviour, helping utilities adjust supply accordingly.

- **Demand Response**: AI signals users to shift usage to off-peak times, reducing stress on the grid and lowering emissions.

- **Fault Detection and Grid Resilience**: AI detects and localises faults in transmission networks, enabling quick response and grid stability.

These capabilities create more flexible, efficient, and sustainable energy systems.

3. Enabling Energy Trading and Decentralisation

AI facilitates new models of energy ownership and exchange:

- **Peer-to-Peer Energy Trading**: AI platforms enable households with solar panels to sell excess energy to neighbours, creating local energy markets.

- **Blockchain Integration**: AI enhances transaction validation and pricing in blockchain-based energy systems.

- **Dynamic Pricing**: AI adjusts electricity prices in real time based on supply and demand, incentivising efficient use.

These innovations empower consumers, support decentralised energy models, and promote sustainability.

Ethical and Practical Considerations

Despite its promise, the application of AI in energy systems poses several challenges:

- **Data Privacy and Security**: Energy usage data is sensitive. AI systems must protect user privacy and guard against cyber threats.

- **Affordability and Access**: Advanced AI solutions may be costly or unavailable in low-income settings. Ensuring inclusive access is crucial.

- **Infrastructure Readiness**: Many regions lack the digital infrastructure needed to support AI-powered systems.

- **Bias and Equity**: Algorithms must avoid reinforcing inequalities by favouring affluent or connected users in energy distribution.

- **Energy Footprint of AI**: Training AI models consumes energy. Sustainable computing practices must be adopted to minimise environmental impact.

Case Studies and Applications

1. Google DeepMind and UK's National Grid

DeepMind partnered with the National Grid to explore

how AI can forecast demand and optimise power generation, aiming to reduce energy waste and emissions.

2. Tesla Powerwall and AutoBidder Tesla's AI-powered AutoBidder platform manages energy storage and trading for Powerwall users, maximising economic returns while stabilising the grid.

3. Schneider Electric EcoStruxure This platform uses AI to manage energy in buildings and industrial facilities, optimising consumption, reducing waste, and lowering carbon footprints.

4. Electrify Network (Singapore) This decentralised energy marketplace uses AI to match producers and consumers, facilitating transparent and efficient energy trading.

5. Okra Solar (Southeast Asia and Africa) Okra uses AI to manage modular solar microgrids in off-grid communities, ensuring reliable and affordable energy access.

Strategies for Scaling AI for SDG 7

1. **Integrate AI into Energy Policy:** National energy strategies should incorporate AI for grid modernisation, decentralisation, and resilience.

2. **Invest in Infrastructure:** Expanding internet access, cloud computing, and sensor networks is essential for enabling smart energy systems.

3. **Support Open Innovation:** Open-source platforms and datasets accelerate the development and localisation of AI energy solutions.

4. **Promote Skills and Training:** Capacity building for energy professionals and communities ensures effective adoption and use.

5. **Encourage Inclusive Business Models:** Subsidies, pay-as-you-go systems, and local manufacturing can make AI-enabled energy accessible to low-income populations.

6. **Ensure Responsible AI Use:** Regulatory frameworks should ensure transparency, accountability, and sustainability in AI energy applications.

AI is redefining the possibilities of clean and affordable energy. By improving forecasting, enhancing storage, optimising distribution, and empowering users, AI plays a central role in accelerating the global energy transition.

When deployed equitably and responsibly, AI can help bridge the energy access gap, reduce emissions, and support climate resilience.

As we strive to meet SDG 7, the fusion of technology and sustainability offers a powerful path forward. But this path must be inclusive, ethical, and grounded in the needs of people and the planet.

Chapter 11:

AI for Decent Work and Economic Growth (SDG 8)

Sustainable Development Goal 8: Decent Work and Economic Growth seeks to promote sustained, inclusive, and sustainable economic growth, full and productive employment, and decent work for all. Economic stability and growth are critical for eradicating poverty, improving living standards, and fostering societal well-being. However, challenges such as unemployment, underemployment, job displacement due to automation, and inequitable access to economic opportunities persist globally.

Artificial Intelligence (AI) has emerged as a transformative tool to address these challenges. By enhancing productivity, fostering innovation, and creating new employment opportunities, AI can significantly contribute to achieving SDG 8. At the same time, it is crucial to address the ethical and social implications of AI adoption to ensure inclusivity and fairness in its impact. This chapter explores how AI can drive economic growth, enable decent work, and promote equitable development worldwide.

AI's Contribution to Economic Growth

1. Enhancing Productivity Across Industries

- **Optimising Operations**: AI-driven tools streamline manufacturing, logistics, and supply chain operations, reducing costs and improving efficiency.

- **Data-Driven Decision Making**: AI analytics enable businesses to make informed decisions, identifying growth opportunities and minimising risks.

- **Innovation in Services**: AI-powered customer service platforms and financial technology (fintech) applications enhance service delivery and user experiences.

2. Driving Innovation and Entrepreneurship

- **Start-up Ecosystems**: AI tools lower barriers for entrepreneurs by providing access to data insights, automating tasks, and enhancing market research.

- **Product Development**: AI accelerates the creation of innovative products and services, from personalised healthcare solutions to sustainable technologies.

- **Access to Capital:** AI-driven credit scoring and investment platforms democratise funding opportunities for small and medium enterprises (SMEs).

3. Developing New Economic Sectors

- **AI-Driven Industries:** The growth of AI-based sectors, such as autonomous systems, advanced robotics, and precision agriculture, creates new economic opportunities.

- **Digital Economies:** AI facilitates the transition to digital economies, enabling e-commerce, online education, and remote work ecosystems.

- **Sustainability Solutions:** AI supports green technologies and circular economies, promoting environmentally sustainable economic growth.

Promoting Decent Work with AI

1. Job Creation Through Technological Advancements

- **AI Development Roles:** Demand for AI developers, data scientists, and machine learning engineers continues to grow.

- **Supportive Ecosystems:** AI fosters the creation of ancillary roles, such as trainers for AI models, data annotators, and ethics specialists.

- **Emerging Professions:** The rise of AI-driven technologies spawns new job categories, such as drone operators, telemedicine specialists, and renewable energy technicians.

2. Upskilling and Reskilling the Workforce

- **AI-Powered Learning Platforms:** Adaptive learning systems provide personalised training programs to help workers acquire new skills. These platforms utilise machine learning algorithms to assess individual progress, identifying strengths and weaknesses to offer tailored content. By creating customised learning pathways, AI ensures that workers can efficiently address skill gaps while building competencies relevant to their roles.

  Virtual learning assistants embedded in these platforms enhance engagement by answering queries in real time, guiding users through complex topics, and providing instant feedback on assignments.

- **Industry-Specific Training**: AI tools deliver targeted upskilling for industries undergoing technological transformation, such as manufacturing and healthcare.

  For instance, AI-powered simulators allow healthcare professionals to practice surgical techniques in a virtual environment, reducing the risks associated with real-world training. In manufacturing, AI analytics help workers adapt to smart factory settings by offering modular training sessions on operating advanced machinery and interpreting sensor data.

  These tools also incorporate gamification elements, such as rewards for completing milestones, to motivate learners and enhance retention.

- **Lifelong Learning Opportunities**: AI enables continuous education, empowering individuals to adapt to evolving job market demands. Through microlearning platforms, workers can access bite-sized courses on emerging technologies, industry trends, and soft skills development.

  AI monitors global employment trends and suggests relevant learning modules, ensuring users stay competitive in dynamic markets.

Additionally, AI facilitates peer-to-peer learning by connecting users with similar goals or expertise, fostering collaborative learning environments that amplify knowledge sharing and innovation.

3. Improving Workplace Conditions

- **Predictive Safety Systems:** AI monitors workplace environments, identifying hazards and preventing accidents.

- **Employee Well-being:** AI-powered mental health and wellness platforms provide support, fostering healthier work environments.

- **Workforce Analytics:** AI analyses employee performance and satisfaction, enabling data-driven improvements in management practices.

Addressing Challenges in AI Adoption

1. Preventing Job Displacement

- **Balancing Automation:** Policies must encourage the use of AI to augment human roles rather than replace them.

- **Inclusive Transition Strategies**: Governments and organisations should implement safety nets, such as unemployment benefits and retraining programs, for workers affected by automation.

- **Public-Private Collaboration**: Joint efforts can create balanced approaches to integrating AI while preserving job opportunities.

2. Ensuring Ethical AI Practices

- **Bias Mitigation**: AI systems must be designed to minimise biases, ensuring fair outcomes in hiring, promotions, and resource allocation.

- **Transparency and Accountability**: Stakeholders must establish standards for explainability and responsibility in AI decision-making processes.

- **Worker Rights Protection**: Policies should safeguard workers' rights in AI-driven workplaces, preventing exploitation and maintaining equitable conditions.

3. Bridging the Digital Divide

- **Infrastructure Development**: Investments in digital infrastructure are essential to ensure access to AI technologies in underserved regions.

- **Affordable Access:** Subsidies and financing models can make AI tools accessible to small businesses and low-income populations.

- **Capacity Building:** Training initiatives should focus on equipping marginalised communities with the skills needed to participate in AI-driven economies.

Strategies for Leveraging AI for SDG 8

1. Policy Frameworks and Regulation

- Governments must establish policies that encourage responsible AI adoption while addressing potential risks such as inequality and job displacement.

- Regulations should incentivise AI innovation in sectors with high potential for job creation and economic growth.

2. Public-Private Partnerships

- Collaborative initiatives between governments, businesses, and non-profits can drive inclusive AI deployment and workforce development.

- Partnerships should focus on fostering innovation hubs, providing funding for AI research, and supporting SMEs in leveraging AI technologies.

3. Promoting Inclusive Innovation

- Stakeholders must ensure that AI solutions address the needs of diverse populations, prioritising equity and inclusion.

- Community engagement programs can provide valuable insights into local challenges and opportunities for AI-driven development.

4. Investing in Research and Education

- Universities and research institutions should collaborate with industries to develop AI curricula and conduct studies on its socio-economic impact.

- Scholarships and grants can promote access to AI education for underrepresented groups, fostering diversity in the field.

Toward a Future of Decent Work and Sustainable Growth

Artificial Intelligence holds immense potential to accelerate economic growth and create decent work opportunities worldwide. By enhancing productivity, fostering innovation, and addressing systemic challenges, AI can contribute significantly to achieving SDG 8.

However, realising this potential requires proactive measures to mitigate risks, ensure inclusivity, and promote ethical practices. Through collaborative efforts, targeted investments, and a commitment to equity, stakeholders can harness AI as a force for sustainable economic development and a future where decent work is accessible to all.

Chapter 12:
AI for Industry, Innovation, and Infrastructure
(SDG 9)

Sustainable Development Goal 9: Industry, Innovation, and Infrastructure promotes inclusive and sustainable industrialisation, fosters innovation, and builds resilient infrastructure. These elements are the backbone of economic development and human well-being.

In an increasingly interconnected and digital world, traditional models of industrial growth and infrastructure development must evolve to meet the demands of sustainability, resilience, and inclusion. Artificial Intelligence (AI) stands out as a transformative technology that can revolutionise industries, modernise infrastructure, and catalyse innovation.

AI's potential to drive SDG 9 lies in its capacity to improve efficiency, enhance decision-making, and foster the development of smart systems across sectors. This chapter explores how AI contributes to sustainable industrialisation through smart manufacturing and AI-driven supply chains, and how predictive analytics powered by AI supports the design and management of resilient infrastructure. It also addresses implementation challenges and proposes strategies to ensure equitable and sustainable adoption.

Smart Manufacturing and AI-Driven Supply Chains

1. Intelligent Automation and Process Optimisation

AI enables a new generation of manufacturing—often referred to as Industry 4.0—characterised by intelligent automation, real-time data analytics, and interconnected systems:

- **Predictive Maintenance:** AI algorithms analyse sensor data to predict equipment failures before they occur, reducing downtime and maintenance costs.
- **Process Optimisation:** Machine learning models adjust production parameters to maximise output, quality, and energy efficiency.

- **Quality Control:** Computer vision systems inspect products for defects with greater accuracy and speed than human workers.

- **Human-Robot Collaboration:** AI enhances robotic systems to safely and efficiently collaborate with humans on assembly lines, increasing flexibility and productivity.

These innovations lead to more efficient, adaptive, and sustainable manufacturing systems.

2. Enhancing Supply Chain Transparency and Resilience

AI transforms supply chains by improving visibility, agility, and responsiveness:

- **Demand Forecasting**: AI predicts consumer demand using historical data, seasonal patterns, and socio-economic trends, helping businesses adjust inventory and reduce waste.

- **Logistics Optimisation**: AI improves route planning, fleet management, and warehouse operations, reducing fuel consumption and delivery times.

- **Risk Management**: AI identifies potential disruptions—such as natural disasters, political instability, or supplier failures—enabling proactive mitigation strategies.

- **Blockchain Integration:** AI combined with blockchain ensures product traceability, combats counterfeiting, and verifies ethical sourcing.

By digitising and connecting the entire supply chain, AI contributes to more sustainable and ethical production and distribution networks.

3. Fostering Innovation and Product Development

AI supports innovation by enabling rapid prototyping, simulation, and design:

- **Generative Design:** AI algorithms generate multiple design alternatives based on defined constraints, often producing innovative and efficient solutions.

- **Digital Twins:** Virtual replicas of physical systems allow engineers to test and optimise products or processes before implementation.

- **Customer-Centred Innovation:** AI analyses customer feedback and market trends to inform product development, enhancing relevance and competitiveness.

These capabilities reduce time-to-market, lower development costs, and increase the likelihood of success.

Building Sustainable Infrastructure with Predictive Analytics

1. Infrastructure Planning and Design

AI enables more informed and sustainable infrastructure development:

- **Site Selection:** AI analyses geographic, demographic, and environmental data to identify optimal locations for roads, schools, hospitals, and utilities.

- **Traffic and Transport Modelling**: AI simulates traffic flows and public transport usage to inform urban planning and reduce congestion.

- **Environmental Impact Assessment**: AI evaluates potential environmental effects of infrastructure projects, supporting compliance and sustainability.

These tools ensure that infrastructure investments are evidence-based, future-ready, and aligned with community needs.

2. Construction Management and Monitoring

AI enhances the efficiency and safety of infrastructure construction and maintenance:

- **Project Scheduling**: AI tools optimise construction timelines and resource allocation to avoid delays and cost overruns.

- **Site Monitoring**: Drones and AI-powered cameras monitor construction progress, worker safety, and regulatory compliance.

- **Structural Health Monitoring**: Sensors embedded in bridges, buildings, and roads provide real-time data on structural integrity, enabling early intervention.

These technologies reduce risks, enhance accountability, and extend infrastructure lifespans.

3. Climate-Resilient Infrastructure

AI helps build infrastructure that can withstand and adapt to climate change:

- **Flood and Disaster Modelling**: AI predicts the impact of extreme weather events on infrastructure and identifies vulnerable areas.

- **Energy-Efficient Systems**: AI controls heating, cooling, and lighting in buildings based on occupancy and external conditions, reducing emissions.

- **Sustainable Materials Research:** AI accelerates the discovery of new construction materials with lower environmental impact.

These applications ensure that infrastructure investments contribute to climate mitigation and adaptation goals.

Ethical and Practical Considerations

Applying AI in industry and infrastructure brings several ethical and operational challenges:

- **Workforce Displacement:** Automation may displace workers in manufacturing and logistics. Reskilling and social protection are essential.

- **Data Governance:** Large-scale use of data requires robust policies for privacy, ownership, and cybersecurity.

- **Bias and Equity:** AI systems must be designed to serve diverse populations and avoid reinforcing existing inequalities.

- **Cost and Accessibility:** Small businesses and low-income countries may struggle to access AI technologies. Inclusive financing and capacity building are needed.

- **Environmental Impact of AI**: The energy consumption of AI systems must be managed to ensure net sustainability gains.

Case Studies and Applications

1. Siemens Digital Industries (Germany) Siemens integrates AI in its smart factories to optimise production, monitor equipment, and reduce energy use. Its MindSphere platform connects machines and systems for real-time analytics.

2. IBM Watson for Supply Chains (Global) IBM's AI platform helps companies detect supply chain disruptions, model alternatives, and improve decision-making.

3. GE's Predix Platform (USA) Predix uses AI to monitor and manage industrial infrastructure, predicting maintenance needs and improving operational efficiency.

4. China's Smart Infrastructure Planning Chinese cities use AI to plan infrastructure investments, integrating data from transportation, energy, and land use to optimise development.

5. Kenya's AI-Enabled Road Monitoring Start-ups in Kenya use AI and smartphone data to detect potholes and monitor road conditions, improving maintenance and safety.

Strategies for Scaling AI for SDG 9

1. **National Innovation Policies:** Governments should develop AI strategies that support sustainable industrialisation and infrastructure development.

2. **Public-Private Collaboration:** Partnerships between governments, businesses, and academic institutions foster innovation ecosystems and scalable solutions.

3. **Support for SMEs:** Providing AI access and support for small and medium enterprises ensures inclusive industrial growth.

4. **Investment in Infrastructure:** Expanding digital infrastructure, including broadband and cloud services, enables AI deployment.

5. **Education and Workforce Development:** Training programmes in AI, engineering, and data science prepare workers for the future of industry.

6. **Ethical Standards and Oversight**: Regulations must ensure transparency, fairness, and accountability in AI applications.

AI offers powerful tools to accelerate sustainable industrialisation, drive innovation, and modernise infrastructure. From smart manufacturing to predictive analytics for construction and logistics, AI enables more efficient, resilient, and inclusive systems.

However, these benefits will only be realised through ethical, inclusive, and context-sensitive implementation.

To meet SDG 9, the integration of AI must be guided by principles of equity, environmental stewardship, and human-centred design. When these principles are embedded, AI becomes not just a technological advancement but a catalyst for a more innovative, sustainable, and connected future.

Chapter 13:
AI for Reducing Inequalities
(SDG 10)

Sustainable Development Goal 10: Reduced Inequalities aims to reduce inequality within and among countries. This includes addressing disparities in income, access to services, opportunities for marginalised groups, and representation in decision-making processes. Despite economic growth in many regions, inequality remains a persistent global challenge, often exacerbated by structural, digital, and economic exclusion.

Artificial Intelligence (AI) presents both risks and opportunities in this context. While AI can entrench existing inequalities through biased algorithms and uneven access, it also offers innovative tools to promote inclusion, empower marginalised communities, and create fairer systems.

This chapter explores how AI can help reduce inequalities through social inclusion tools and by addressing economic and digital divides. It also examines ethical concerns and outlines strategies to ensure that AI development and deployment are equitable, inclusive, and globally beneficial.

AI-Powered Social Inclusion Tools

1. Enhancing Access to Services for Marginalised Groups

AI can improve access to public services, health, education, and social protection for historically underserved populations:

- **Multilingual Interfaces**: AI-powered translation and natural language processing tools enable access to services in indigenous and minority languages.

- **Accessibility Tools**: AI facilitates communication and learning for people with disabilities through text-to-speech, speech-to-text, sign language recognition, and facial expression interpretation.

- **Personalised Public Services**: AI tailors services based on user needs, such as personalised healthcare, benefits eligibility, and education support for disadvantaged learners.

- **Chatbots and Virtual Assistants**: These tools provide low-cost, round-the-clock support for accessing government and legal services, particularly in rural and underserved areas.

These applications reduce barriers to participation and ensure more people can engage with and benefit from public systems.

2. Empowering Marginalised Voices

AI can amplify the voices of marginalised communities and enable greater civic participation:

- **Sentiment Analysis and Social Listening:** AI analyses public opinion and social media discussions to identify concerns and needs of vulnerable groups.

- **Participatory Platforms:** AI enhances digital democracy platforms by analysing citizen feedback and making recommendations for policy development.

- **Bias Detection in Media and Content:** AI tools detect discriminatory language and representation in media, promoting more inclusive narratives.

These tools ensure that policy, media, and social systems are more responsive and representative.

3. Supporting Human Rights and Advocacy

AI can assist in identifying and addressing rights violations:

- **Monitoring Discrimination and Hate Speech:** AI identifies patterns of abuse in online platforms, helping moderators respond to hate speech, racism, and sexism.

- **Predictive Policing Accountability:** AI can also be used to audit and reform biased policing systems, ensuring that enforcement does not disproportionately target marginalised groups.

- **Access to Legal Aid:** AI tools provide legal information and case analysis for individuals who cannot afford legal representation.

AI used responsibly in these contexts strengthens justice systems and safeguards human rights.

Addressing Economic and Digital Divides

1. Promoting Digital Inclusion

The digital divide prevents millions from accessing the benefits of AI and digital services. Bridging this divide is essential for inclusive AI:

- **Low-Cost Devices and Platforms:** AI can run on low-bandwidth devices and offline platforms, enabling access in areas with limited infrastructure.

- **Digital Literacy Programmes**: AI-driven educational tools can teach digital and financial literacy to adults and young people in marginalised communities.

- **Community Wi-Fi and Connectivity**: AI helps optimise the deployment of connectivity infrastructure by identifying underserved areas.

Reducing the digital divide ensures that everyone can participate in and benefit from digital economies.

2. Inclusive Labour Market Interventions

AI has the potential to support inclusive employment and entrepreneurship:

- **Job Matching Platforms**: AI platforms connect job seekers from disadvantaged backgrounds with opportunities suited to their skills and locations.

- **Reskilling and Upskilling**: AI-driven learning platforms offer personalised training for individuals affected by automation or economic disruption.

- **Inclusive Hiring Practices**: AI tools can anonymise applications and flag biased hiring patterns, promoting diversity and fairness in recruitment.

- **Microenterprise Support**: AI assists small business owners with market research, financial planning, and accessing digital tools.

These interventions can create new pathways to economic empowerment for marginalised communities.

3. Equitable Financial Services
AI supports financial inclusion and economic participation for underbanked populations:

- **Alternative Credit Scoring**: AI analyses mobile phone usage, social media data, and transaction histories to offer credit to those without formal banking history.

- **Fraud Detection**: AI enhances security in financial systems, increasing trust among underserved users.

- **Mobile Financial Services**: AI chatbots and digital wallets expand access to banking and savings in low-income and rural areas.

These services reduce financial exclusion and support entrepreneurship.

Ethical and Practical Considerations

AI for inequality reduction must be designed and deployed with care:

- **Bias and Discrimination:** AI systems trained on skewed data can replicate or worsen inequalities. Fairness-aware AI and regular audits are essential.

- **Data Privacy:** Collecting and analysing data on marginalised communities must respect their privacy and autonomy.

- **Representation in Design:** Involving affected communities in AI design ensures relevance and accountability.

- **Affordability and Access:** AI tools must be affordable and usable for the people they aim to support.

- **Sustainability:** Solutions should be scalable and maintainable in low-resource settings.

Without these safeguards, AI could deepen rather than reduce inequalities.

Case Studies and Applications

1. EqualAI (USA) EqualAI works to identify and eliminate bias in AI systems through audits, education, and policy development, promoting inclusive AI practices.

2. Hello World (Uganda and UK) This initiative deploys solar-powered digital hubs with AI-based learning content in remote communities, fostering digital and educational inclusion.

3. CreditEnable (India) Using AI to assess the creditworthiness of small businesses with limited formal records, this platform supports financial inclusion and entrepreneurship.

4. uLesson (Nigeria) An edtech platform providing AI-personalised learning for students in West Africa, including offline access for rural learners.

5. AI4Good Lab (Canada) This lab supports women and minorities in developing AI solutions for social challenges, building capacity and representation in the field.

Strategies for Scaling AI for SDG 10

1. **Inclusive AI Policy Frameworks:** National strategies should prioritise fairness, access, and equity in AI development and deployment.

2. **Investment in Local Innovation:** Supporting grassroots innovators and start-ups ensures context-appropriate and inclusive AI solutions.

3. **Public-Private-Civil Society Collaboration:** Multi-stakeholder partnerships help align technological development with social justice goals.

4. **Capacity Building and Education:** Expanding AI literacy among marginalised groups ensures they are not just recipients but shapers of technology.

5. **Open-Source and Interoperable Tools:** Encouraging the development and sharing of open-source AI tools promotes accessibility and transparency.

6. **Monitoring and Impact Evaluation:** Regular assessments of AI tools' impact on inequality help refine and scale successful models.

AI can be a powerful force for inclusion and equality if developed and deployed thoughtfully. From expanding access to services and promoting civic participation to bridging digital divides and enabling economic opportunities, AI offers practical tools for reducing disparities within and among countries.

However, these benefits are not guaranteed. Without deliberate design and ethical governance, AI may exacerbate the very inequalities it seeks to solve. The future of AI and SDG 10 lies in our collective commitment to equity, representation, and justice.

By ensuring that marginalised communities are at the centre of AI development and benefit fully from its applications, we can harness this technology to create a fairer and more inclusive world.

Chapter 14:
AI for Sustainable Cities and Communities (SDG 11)

Sustainable Development Goal 11: Sustainable Cities and Communities aims to make cities inclusive, safe, resilient, and sustainable. With more than half the world's population living in urban areas and projections suggesting that this will rise to nearly 70% by 2050, cities are at the forefront of global sustainability challenges. Rapid urbanisation places pressure on infrastructure, housing, transportation, public services, and the environment. At the same time, cities are hubs of innovation, economic activity, and cultural exchange.

Artificial Intelligence (AI) is reshaping how cities are planned, governed, and experienced. From optimising traffic flows and managing energy consumption to enhancing disaster preparedness and ensuring equitable service delivery, AI offers transformative potential for urban resilience and sustainability. This chapter explores how AI contributes to achieving SDG 11 through smart city development, urban planning, and AI-driven disaster management systems, while addressing challenges related to privacy, equity, and infrastructure.

Smart Cities and Urban Planning

1. Enhancing Urban Infrastructure and Services

AI powers intelligent infrastructure and service delivery systems:

- **Traffic Management:** AI analyses traffic patterns in real time to optimise signal timing, reduce congestion, and improve air quality.

- **Smart Lighting and Utilities:** AI-controlled lighting adjusts brightness based on time of day and occupancy, saving energy and reducing emissions.

- **Waste Management:** AI predicts waste generation, optimises collection routes, and detects illegal dumping through sensor networks and image recognition.

- **Water and Energy Management:** AI forecasts consumption patterns, detects leaks, and automates billing systems for efficient resource use.

These systems enhance operational efficiency, reduce environmental impact, and improve quality of life.

2. Data-Driven Urban Planning

Urban planning increasingly relies on AI to support evidence-based decisions:

- **Land Use and Zoning Analysis**: AI analyses satellite imagery, demographic trends, and land use data to inform urban zoning decisions.

- **Affordable Housing Development**: AI identifies optimal locations for housing developments by evaluating access to transport, services, and jobs.

- **Social Equity Mapping**: AI integrates census, economic, and environmental data to highlight disparities in infrastructure and service provision.

- **Public Transport Optimisation**: AI models passenger flow and demand to redesign transit routes and schedules for maximum coverage and efficiency.

AI allows planners to visualise future scenarios, test policies, and ensure inclusive urban growth.

3. Citizen Engagement and Governance

AI fosters greater public participation and more responsive urban governance:

- **Chatbots and Virtual Assistants**: AI tools provide city information, process service requests, and answer citizens' questions around the clock.

- **Sentiment Analysis and Public Feedback**: AI analyses social media and community input to gauge satisfaction and identify areas for improvement.

- **Participatory Budgeting Platforms**: AI helps city governments collect and prioritise public suggestions for local investment and planning.

These tools build transparency, trust, and collaboration between residents and authorities.

AI-Driven Disaster Management Systems

1. Predictive Analytics and Early Warning Systems
AI strengthens urban resilience by enabling early detection and response to disasters:

- **Weather and Hazard Forecasting**: AI models analyse meteorological, geological, and environmental data to predict floods, storms, earthquakes, and heatwaves.

- **Urban Risk Mapping**: AI identifies high-risk zones based on infrastructure quality, population density, and historical incident data.

- **Evacuation Planning**: AI simulates disaster scenarios to design efficient evacuation routes and emergency response plans.

These systems reduce loss of life, economic disruption, and infrastructure damage.

2. Emergency Response and Recovery
AI supports rapid and effective crisis response:

- **Drone and Satellite Surveillance**: AI analyses real-time imagery to assess damage, locate survivors, and coordinate rescue operations.

- **Resource Allocation**: AI determines the optimal deployment of emergency services, supplies, and personnel based on evolving conditions.

- **Infrastructure Monitoring**: Sensors and AI detect structural weaknesses in buildings, bridges, and roads, ensuring safety post-disaster.

Post-crisis, AI also helps assess impacts, manage reconstruction, and build future resilience.

3. Climate Adaptation and Urban Resilience
AI supports long-term strategies for climate adaptation in urban areas:

- **Urban Heat Island Mapping**: AI detects temperature variations and recommends interventions like green roofs and tree planting.

- **Flood Mitigation Planning**: AI models stormwater flows and designs resilient drainage systems to prevent urban flooding.

- **Building Code Optimisation**: AI evaluates the performance of construction standards under future climate scenarios, informing policy reforms.

These tools ensure cities adapt to changing climate conditions while safeguarding communities.

Ethical and Practical Considerations

Implementing AI in cities must be guided by ethical principles and practical constraints:

- **Data Privacy and Surveillance Risks:** Smart cities collect vast amounts of data. Strong governance is needed to prevent misuse and protect privacy.

- **Digital Inequality:** Not all residents have equal access to smart city technologies. Inclusion must be central to planning and design.

- **Algorithmic Bias**: AI systems may reflect and reinforce social biases if not properly designed and tested.

- **Cybersecurity**: As cities become more connected, they become more vulnerable to cyberattacks. Robust defences are critical.

- **Public Trust and Transparency**: Citizens must be informed about how data is used and have a say in how AI systems operate in public life.

Case Studies and Applications

1. Barcelona's Smart City Model (Spain) Barcelona uses AI to manage water systems, monitor pollution, and operate a city-wide sensor network for urban services. The city prioritises data sovereignty and citizen participation.

2. SmartDhaka Initiative (Bangladesh) Dhaka is deploying AI for traffic management, waste collection, and public transport improvements, focusing on affordability and accessibility.

3. FEMA and AI for Disaster Response (USA) The Federal Emergency Management Agency uses AI to model disaster scenarios and allocate resources more effectively across communities.

4. Tokyo's Disaster Prevention System (Japan) AI monitors seismic activity and coordinates emergency communication systems to prepare for earthquakes and tsunamis.

5. Kigali's Smart Bus System (Rwanda) AI optimises routes and fare collection for Kigali's bus rapid transit system, improving accessibility and service quality.

Strategies for Scaling AI for SDG 11

1. **Inclusive Urban Policy Frameworks:** Governments should develop smart city strategies that align AI deployment with social, environmental, and economic objectives.

2. **Digital Infrastructure Investment:** Expanding internet access, sensor networks, and cloud services is critical for effective AI integration.

3. **Public-Private-Civic Collaboration:** Cities should partner with tech firms, researchers, and community organisations to ensure responsible innovation.

4. **Open Data and Interoperability:** Open-source platforms and data-sharing standards promote transparency and scalability.

5. **Urban AI Literacy:** Educating city officials, planners, and citizens about AI builds capacity and supports participatory governance.

6. **Monitoring and Evaluation Systems:** Continuous assessment ensures AI tools meet sustainability and equity goals and adapt to changing needs.

Artificial Intelligence has the potential to transform cities into inclusive, efficient, and resilient environments. Whether by optimising infrastructure, improving public services, or preparing for disasters, AI contributes to the vision of sustainable urban living. However, these benefits can only be realised if AI is implemented transparently, inclusively, and ethically.

As urbanisation accelerates, integrating AI into city planning and management is not just a technological imperative—it is a social and environmental necessity. When guided by human values and grounded in the real needs of communities, AI can help create cities that are not only smarter but also fairer and more sustainable for all.

Chapter 15:
AI for Responsible Consumption and Production
(SDG 12)

Sustainable Development Goal 12: Responsible Consumption and Production aims to ensure sustainable patterns of consumption and production, encouraging efficiency, minimising waste, and promoting circular economies. As global consumption continues to rise, environmental degradation, resource depletion, and waste generation pose serious threats to planetary health and human well-being. Achieving SDG 12 requires systemic change in how goods and services are produced, used, and disposed of.

Artificial Intelligence (AI) provides powerful tools to drive these transformations. With its ability to collect and analyse large datasets, identify inefficiencies, and optimise decision-making in real time, AI enables smarter resource use and sustainable production methods.

This chapter explores how AI supports SDG 12 by reducing waste, optimising resource use, and enabling circular economy solutions. It also considers ethical considerations and outlines strategies for scaling responsible AI use across industries.

Reducing Waste and Optimising Resource Use

1. Predictive Analytics in Supply Chains

AI helps producers and retailers forecast demand and reduce overproduction and waste:

- **Demand Forecasting**: AI models analyse historical data, consumer trends, and external factors (e.g. weather, holidays) to predict demand with high accuracy.

- **Inventory Management**: AI tracks inventory levels and shelf life in real time, automating restocking and preventing spoilage or obsolescence.

- **Smart Procurement**: AI recommends optimal purchase quantities and timing, reducing excess material purchases.

These tools cut down on overstocking, reduce emissions from unnecessary production, and minimise disposal costs.

2. Sustainable Manufacturing and Product Design

AI enhances the efficiency of production processes and supports eco-friendly design:

- **Process Optimisation:** Machine learning identifies inefficiencies in manufacturing processes and recommends improvements to reduce energy, water, and material consumption.

- **Material Selection:** AI analyses environmental and performance data to recommend sustainable alternatives to traditional materials.

- **Eco-Design Tools:** Generative design algorithms create products that use fewer resources, are easier to recycle, and generate less waste.

These applications contribute to greener production methods and more sustainable consumption patterns.

3. Reducing Food Waste

Food waste accounts for significant environmental harm. AI can address this at multiple stages:

- **Smart Fridges and Retail Systems:** AI tracks expiry dates and usage patterns to reduce spoilage in homes and supermarkets.

- **Supply Chain Efficiency:** AI monitors food quality during transport and storage, identifying risks and reducing loss.

- **Surplus Redistribution:** Platforms use AI to match surplus food from producers and retailers with food banks and charities in real time.

Reducing food waste contributes to climate mitigation and supports food security.

Circular Economy Solutions Powered by AI

1. Product Life Cycle Management

AI supports circularity by tracking and extending the life cycle of products:

- **Usage Monitoring:** IoT and AI systems monitor product use and performance, providing insights for repair, reuse, or resale.

- **Predictive Maintenance:** AI forecasts when maintenance is needed, preventing premature failure and reducing waste.

- **End-of-Life Management:** AI identifies optimal disposal or recycling options based on material composition and condition.

These strategies promote reuse, remanufacturing, and recycling, closing the material loop.

2. Intelligent Recycling and Waste Sorting

AI automates and improves waste sorting and recycling systems:

- **Computer Vision for Sorting**: AI systems in recycling facilities use image recognition to sort waste accurately by material type, improving recycling rates.

- **Smart Bins**: Equipped with AI, these bins identify the type of waste deposited and guide users on proper disposal.

- **Recycling Market Analytics**: AI analyses recycling trends and market prices, helping recyclers make data-driven decisions about processing and sales.

These innovations reduce landfill use, increase recycling efficiency, and enhance the economic viability of circular models.

3. Resource Sharing and Product-as-a-Service Models

AI enables new consumption models that prioritise access over ownership:

- **Sharing Platforms**: AI matches users with shared resources—such as vehicles, tools, or office space—based on location, availability, and preferences.

- **Product-as-a-Service (PaaS)**: AI manages usage, maintenance, and billing for services like leased appliances, electronics, and industrial equipment.

- **Lifecycle Tracking**: AI tracks the use and performance of shared assets, informing upgrades, reuse, or recycling at the right time.

These models reduce resource consumption and promote sustainable lifestyles.

Ethical and Practical Considerations

The use of AI in consumption and production systems raises important ethical and operational issues:

- **Data Privacy and Ownership**: Users of smart appliances or shared services must retain control over their personal and usage data.

- **Digital Divide**: Small businesses and low-income consumers may lack access to AI-enabled tools, risking exclusion from sustainability benefits.

- **Algorithmic Transparency:** Consumers and regulators must understand how AI makes decisions—e.g. recommending products or adjusting supply chains.

- **Labour Impacts:** Automation may displace workers in manufacturing and logistics. Reskilling and social protections are essential.

- **Environmental Cost of AI:** AI itself consumes energy and materials. Sustainable computing practices are necessary to ensure net positive impact.

Addressing these issues is essential to ensure that AI supports responsible consumption equitably.

Case Studies and Applications

1. Winnow (UK): Winnow uses AI-powered scales and analytics to track food waste in commercial kitchens, helping chefs reduce waste and save money.

2. AMP Robotics (USA) AMP Robotics develops AI-driven systems for sorting recyclable materials in waste facilities, improving accuracy and throughput.

3. Circularise (Netherlands) This platform uses AI and blockchain to trace materials across supply chains, enabling transparency and circular product design.

4. Too Good To Go (Europe) An AI-driven app that connects consumers with surplus food from restaurants and retailers at discounted prices, reducing waste and emissions.

5. IKEA and AI for Circularity: IKEA uses AI to analyse customer feedback and product returns to design longer-lasting, repairable products and expand resale and recycling schemes.

Strategies for Scaling AI for SDG 12

1. **Sustainable AI Design:** Developers must prioritise energy efficiency and sustainability in AI model training and deployment.

2. **Policy and Regulation:** Governments should adopt policies that incentivise circular economy models and ensure transparency in AI-driven decision-making.

3. **Capacity Building:** Supporting SMEs and communities with training and access to AI tools ensures inclusive participation in sustainable production.

4. **Collaboration Across Sectors:** Partnerships between tech companies, manufacturers, governments, and civil society accelerate innovation and scale.

5. **Open Data and Standards:** Sharing data and creating standards for sustainability metrics support accountability and interoperability.

6. **Consumer Awareness and Participation:** Educating consumers about AI-enabled sustainability choices fosters responsible consumption habits.

AI is a powerful enabler of responsible consumption and production. From reducing waste and improving supply chains to enabling new business models and circular systems, AI can drive the transition to a more sustainable economy. However, its success depends on inclusive access, ethical design, and alignment with broader sustainability goals.

Achieving SDG 12 with AI requires collaboration, innovation, and a commitment to equity and environmental stewardship. With the right frameworks in place, AI can help create production and consumption systems that are not only efficient and profitable but also sustainable and just.

Chapter 16:
AI for Climate Action
(SDG 13)

Sustainable Development Goal 13: Climate Action calls for urgent efforts to combat climate change and its impacts. Climate change is a defining global challenge of our time, with consequences including rising sea levels, extreme weather events, biodiversity loss, and threats to food and water security. Tackling these challenges requires global cooperation, robust data analysis, predictive models, and proactive mitigation strategies.

Artificial Intelligence (AI) has emerged as a vital tool in understanding and addressing climate change. With its capacity to analyse complex datasets, simulate future scenarios, and optimise systems, AI empowers decision-makers and communities to take more informed, effective climate actions.

This chapter explores how AI contributes to climate modelling and forecasting, and how it mitigates environmental impacts through intelligent technologies. It also considers ethical concerns and strategies for equitable AI implementation in climate efforts.

Climate Modelling and Forecasting

1. Climate Data Analysis and Integration

AI enables more accurate and timely insights by processing vast amounts of environmental data:

- **Satellite and Remote Sensing Data**: AI analyses imagery and sensor data from satellites to monitor changes in vegetation, ice cover, ocean temperatures, and emissions.

- **Climate Record Integration**: Machine learning integrates disparate climate data sources—historical records, observational data, and sensor networks—into coherent, actionable insights.

- **Gap Filling and Error Correction**: AI fills gaps in climate datasets and corrects anomalies, improving the reliability of modelling efforts.

These capabilities ensure a better understanding of the current state of the planet and guide science-based climate policy.

2. Advanced Climate Modelling

AI supports the development of sophisticated models that simulate climate systems:

- **Global Climate Models (GCMs):** AI enhances the performance of GCMs by reducing computational requirements while increasing resolution and precision.

- **Downscaling Models:** AI translates global models into localised predictions, providing region-specific data for cities and communities.

- **Probabilistic Forecasting:** Machine learning enables ensemble modelling, improving uncertainty estimates and risk assessment.

Such models inform long-term planning for infrastructure, agriculture, water management, and disaster preparedness.

3. Weather and Disaster Forecasting

AI improves the speed and accuracy of short- and medium-term forecasts:

- **Extreme Weather Prediction:** AI models forecast events like hurricanes, droughts, floods, and wildfires, enabling early warning systems.

- **Real-Time Monitoring:** AI monitors environmental indicators to trigger alerts and guide rapid response.

- **Seasonal Forecasting**: AI supports the prediction of monsoons, El Niño patterns, and other seasonal shifts critical to agriculture and water management.

These tools protect lives and livelihoods by enabling timely and targeted interventions.

Mitigating Environmental Impacts Using AI Technologies

1. Reducing Greenhouse Gas Emissions

AI helps reduce emissions across sectors by optimising resource use and improving energy systems:

- **Smart Grid Management:** AI balances energy supply and demand, integrates renewable sources, and reduces reliance on fossil fuels.

- **Emission Tracking and Reporting**: AI monitors emissions from transport, industry, and agriculture, supporting carbon accounting and regulatory compliance.

- **Sustainable Mobility:** AI enables dynamic traffic management, route optimisation, and public transport planning to cut transport emissions.

These technologies support national and corporate decarbonisation strategies.

2. Climate-Smart Agriculture

AI enables more sustainable and resilient agricultural practices:

- **Precision Farming**: AI guides irrigation, fertiliser application, and planting schedules based on soil, weather, and crop data, reducing resource use and emissions.

- **Yield Prediction and Risk Management**: AI forecasts crop performance and identifies vulnerabilities, helping farmers adapt to climate risks.

- **Land Use Optimisation**: AI assesses land suitability for different crops, enabling shifts toward less climate-intensive production systems.

These practices boost productivity while minimising environmental harm.

3. Ecosystem Monitoring and Restoration

AI supports conservation and ecosystem management:

- **Deforestation Detection:** AI analyses satellite imagery to identify illegal logging and habitat destruction in near real-time.

- **Biodiversity Monitoring**: AI processes audio, video, and image data to track species and detect changes in ecosystem health.

- **Reforestation Planning**: AI identifies optimal reforestation sites based on soil, climate, and biodiversity data.

These tools preserve carbon sinks, protect biodiversity, and maintain ecosystem services.

4. Green Infrastructure and Urban Planning

AI facilitates sustainable infrastructure development:

- **Urban Heat Island Mitigation:** AI identifies hotspots and recommends green roofs, vegetation cover, and reflective surfaces.

- **Energy-Efficient Building Design:** AI optimises heating, ventilation, and lighting systems for reduced energy consumption.

- **Sustainable Transportation Planning**: AI informs the design of pedestrian and cycling infrastructure to reduce emissions.

These interventions enhance climate resilience and reduce urban environmental impact.

Ethical and Practical Considerations

Applying AI to climate action must address several critical issues:

- **Data Accessibility**: Many low-income regions lack access to the data needed for effective AI applications. Data sharing and capacity building are essential.

- **Algorithmic Transparency**: AI models must be interpretable and transparent to ensure accountability and trust.

- **Equity and Justice**: AI solutions must serve vulnerable communities that are most affected by climate change, not just affluent users or nations.

- **Sustainability of AI**: AI training and infrastructure require significant energy. Green computing practices are necessary to reduce AI's carbon footprint.

- **Global Collaboration:** Climate change is a global problem. International cooperation is needed to ensure equitable access to AI tools and knowledge.

Case Studies and Applications

1. Climate TRACE (Global): A global coalition using AI to track greenhouse gas emissions from satellite imagery and public datasets, providing transparent data for policy and advocacy.

2. IBM Green Horizons (China): AI models developed with the Chinese government help forecast air pollution and inform urban emission reduction policies.

3. Microsoft's AI for Earth (Global): This programme funds and supports AI-based solutions for land use, biodiversity, water, and climate modelling across multiple countries.

4. Google DeepMind Weather Prediction (UK): DeepMind developed AI models capable of forecasting precipitation and weather patterns more accurately than traditional models in some cases.

5. PlanetWatchers (Global): This AI platform uses satellite data to monitor land use and deforestation, supporting conservation efforts and carbon credit verification.

Strategies for Scaling AI for SDG 13

1. **Policy Integration**: National climate strategies should incorporate AI as a core tool for forecasting, mitigation, and adaptation.

2. **Open Data and Tools**: Governments and organisations should invest in open-access climate datasets and AI platforms for global use.

3. **Capacity Building**: Training scientists, policymakers, and communities in AI and data literacy enhances local resilience and innovation.

4. **Ethical AI Governance**: Regulatory frameworks should ensure fairness, transparency, and sustainability in AI development and deployment.

5. **Cross-Sector Collaboration**: Partnerships among tech firms, academia, NGOs, and governments accelerate innovation and deployment.

6. **Monitoring and Impact Evaluation**: Rigorous assessment of AI tools helps measure climate impact and guides continuous improvement.

AI is a critical enabler of effective climate action. By improving climate modelling, forecasting extreme events, reducing emissions, and guiding adaptation efforts, AI enhances humanity's ability to respond to the climate crisis. Yet to truly fulfil this promise, AI must be deployed ethically, inclusively, and sustainably.

Real progress on SDG 13 requires integrating AI with bold climate policy, strong global cooperation, and local empowerment. With the right frameworks in place, AI can help societies anticipate, adapt to, and mitigate the impacts of climate change—safeguarding both people and the planet.

Chapter 17:
AI for Life Below Water
(SDG 14)

Sustainable Development Goal 14: Life Below Water aims to conserve and sustainably use the oceans, seas, and marine resources. Oceans cover over 70% of the Earth's surface and play a critical role in regulating climate, supporting biodiversity, and providing food and livelihoods for billions. However, marine ecosystems face increasing threats from overfishing, pollution, habitat loss, and climate change.

These pressures jeopardise both environmental health and economic resilience in coastal communities.

Artificial Intelligence (AI) offers innovative tools to support marine conservation, monitor ocean health, and foster sustainable fishing. With its capacity to process vast amounts of spatial and environmental data, AI empowers governments, researchers, and communities to take informed and timely actions to protect oceanic ecosystems.

This chapter explores how AI supports SDG 14 through AI-powered marine monitoring and predictive analytics for sustainable fisheries. It also highlights ethical considerations and strategies for inclusive, data-driven ocean stewardship.

Marine Conservation through AI-Powered Monitoring

1. Ocean Health Monitoring

AI strengthens the capacity to observe and assess marine environments:

- **Remote Sensing and Satellite Imagery**: AI analyses satellite data to monitor changes in sea surface temperature, coral bleaching, algal blooms, and ocean acidification.

- **Underwater Sensor Networks**: AI processes data from autonomous underwater vehicles (AUVs), buoys, and sonar systems to detect pollutants, noise levels, and biodiversity shifts.

- **Acoustic Monitoring**: Machine learning identifies marine species and tracks migration patterns by analysing underwater acoustic signals.

These technologies offer real-time insights and early warnings for conservation efforts.

2. Coral Reef and Habitat Protection

Coral reefs are vital yet vulnerable ecosystems. AI supports their protection by:

- **Coral Health Assessment**: Computer vision analyses images of coral reefs to detect disease, bleaching, and regrowth.

- **Habitat Mapping**: AI integrates oceanographic and visual data to create high-resolution maps of seafloor habitats and biodiversity hotspots.

- **Impact Analysis**: AI evaluates the effects of tourism, fishing, and climate change on reef ecosystems, informing mitigation strategies.

These tools enable targeted interventions and adaptive marine management.

3. Pollution Detection and Mitigation

AI detects marine pollution and guides clean-up efforts:

- **Plastic Waste Tracking**: AI identifies floating plastic debris via satellite and drone imagery, predicting movement based on ocean currents and weather patterns.

- **Oil Spill Detection**: AI processes radar and thermal imagery to identify oil spills, estimate their spread, and assess impact on marine life.

- **Wastewater and Chemical Discharge Monitoring**: AI analyses environmental sensor data to trace and quantify land-based pollutants entering coastal waters.

This supports more effective enforcement of pollution regulations and remediation planning.

Predictive Analytics for Sustainable Fishing Practices

1. Fish Population Monitoring
   Sustainable fisheries rely on accurate data about fish stocks:
- **Species Recognition**: AI identifies fish species from images or video footage collected at ports, markets, and on-board vessels.

- **Population Estimation**: Machine learning analyses acoustic and visual survey data to estimate stock levels and population dynamics.

- **Illegal, Unreported, and Unregulated (IUU) Fishing Detection**: AI detects suspicious vessel behaviours using Automatic Identification System (AIS) data and satellite imagery.

This helps regulators set quotas, enforce rules, and prevent overfishing.

2. Sustainable Catch Optimisation

AI supports fishing practices that are both productive and sustainable:

- **Bycatch Reduction:** AI identifies fishing conditions likely to result in bycatch and recommends alternative gear, timing, or locations.

- **Fishing Effort Optimisation:** AI tools predict optimal fishing zones, minimising fuel use and environmental disruption.

- **Dynamic Fishery Management:** AI informs real-time policy adjustments based on environmental and market conditions.

These tools align conservation goals with economic sustainability

3. Supply Chain Transparency and Traceability

AI ensures traceability from ocean to market:

- **Blockchain Integration:** AI supports secure data logging on fish origins, handling, and transit conditions.

- **Smart Labelling:** AI-generated QR codes provide consumers with detailed sustainability and safety information.

- **Market Forecasting:** AI analyses demand trends and pricing, helping fishers plan harvests and reduce waste.

This builds consumer trust and rewards sustainable practices.

Ethical and Practical Considerations

Deploying AI in ocean governance requires attention to fairness, inclusion, and sustainability:

- **Data Sovereignty:** Indigenous and coastal communities must retain ownership over local marine data.

- **Equity and Access:** Tools must be accessible to small-scale fishers and marine conservationists in low-income regions.

- **Environmental Costs**: AI deployment must consider its energy and material footprint, especially in marine hardware.

- **Transparency and Trust**: AI models must be interpretable to ensure stakeholders trust and act on their outputs.

- **Cultural Sensitivity**: AI solutions should respect traditional knowledge and fishing practices, integrating them into modern approaches.

These principles ensure AI serves as a tool of empowerment rather than exclusion.

Case Studies and Applications

1. Global Fishing Watch (International) Uses AI to process satellite data and monitor fishing activities globally, detecting illegal and unregulated fishing in near real-time.

2. CoralNet (Global) An AI-powered platform for analysing coral reef images, used by researchers and marine park managers to monitor reef health.

3. OceanMind (UK) Applies AI to track fishing vessels, assess compliance with regulations, and provide governments with enforcement tools.

4. DeepSea Coral Atlas (USA) AI analyses ROV imagery to map deep-sea coral habitats, supporting marine protected area planning and conservation.

5. Spot the Jellyfish (Malta) A citizen science app powered by AI that helps researchers track jellyfish blooms and understand ecosystem changes.

Strategies for Scaling AI for SDG 14

1. **Support Open Ocean Data Initiatives**: Making marine datasets publicly accessible accelerates innovation and transparency.

2. **Invest in Coastal Digital Infrastructure**: Expanding internet and sensor networks enables more effective AI deployment.

3. **Empower Coastal Communities**: Training and resources for local fishers and conservationists support adoption and ownership of AI tools.

4. **Cross-Border Collaboration**: Regional and international cooperation ensures coordinated action on shared marine challenges.

5. **Develop Ethical AI Guidelines**: Frameworks for responsible use ensure AI systems respect ecological and social values.

6. **Monitor and Evaluate Impact**: Continuous feedback loops help assess the effectiveness of AI in achieving conservation and sustainability outcomes.

AI presents a powerful means to monitor, protect, and sustainably use marine resources. From real-time ocean monitoring and pollution detection to predictive fishery analytics and supply chain transparency, AI enables data-driven stewardship of life below water.

But its benefits can only be fully realised through inclusive access, ethical governance, and a commitment to equity and environmental justice.

To meet SDG 14, we must embed AI into marine policy and practice as a tool for empowerment, sustainability, and resilience. The health of our oceans—and the billions of people who depend on them depends on how wisely we wield this powerful technology.

Chapter 18:
AI for Life on Land
(SDG 15)

Sustainable Development Goal 15: Life on Land calls for the protection, restoration, and sustainable use of terrestrial ecosystems, forests, mountains, and biodiversity. Terrestrial ecosystems provide essential services, including air purification, carbon storage, food, and water, and serve as habitats for countless species. However, human activities such as deforestation, land degradation, desertification, and habitat destruction have severely impacted biodiversity and ecosystem resilience.

Artificial Intelligence (AI) has emerged as a transformative tool in addressing these environmental challenges. By enabling more accurate monitoring, real-time decision-making, and predictive modelling, AI enhances our ability to conserve biodiversity, manage land resources sustainably, and combat environmental degradation.

This chapter explores how AI supports SDG 15 through biodiversity tracking, forest management, land use planning, and ecosystem restoration, while also examining ethical considerations and strategies for equitable implementation.

Biodiversity Monitoring and Conservation

1. Species Identification and Tracking

AI helps researchers identify and monitor plant and animal species more efficiently:

- **Computer Vision for Wildlife Recognition**: AI-powered image and video analysis tools identify species captured by camera traps and drones, reducing manual processing time.

- **Bioacoustic Monitoring**: Machine learning models detect species-specific sounds in forests and grasslands, tracking bird calls, insect activity, and mammal movements.

- **Movement Tracking**: AI analyses GPS collar data to monitor migration patterns, habitat use, and threats to endangered species.

These tools provide critical data for conservation planning and habitat protection.

2. Habitat and Ecosystem Health Assessment

AI evaluates the condition of terrestrial ecosystems:

- **Remote Sensing Analysis**: AI interprets satellite images to assess vegetation cover, soil moisture, and land degradation.

- **Ecological Modelling**: AI simulates ecosystem interactions and responses to climate or human pressure, informing intervention strategies.

- **Invasive Species Detection**: AI identifies non-native species in agricultural or wild landscapes through image recognition and environmental DNA analysis.

These insights enable timely and informed ecosystem management.

Forest Management and Land Use Planning

1. Forest Monitoring and Deforestation Prevention

Forests are key to carbon sequestration and biodiversity.

AI supports their conservation by:

- **Illegal Logging Detection**: AI analyses satellite data and audio sensors to detect chainsaw activity, road building, and forest encroachment.

- **Deforestation Mapping**: AI monitors tree loss in near real-time, identifying trends and hotspots for targeted interventions.

- **Forest Fire Prediction**: AI models assess fire risk using weather, vegetation, and topography data, guiding prevention efforts.

These tools support enforcement agencies and conservation groups in protecting critical forest areas.

2. Land Use Optimisation and Sustainable Agriculture

AI guides sustainable land allocation and agricultural practices:

- **Crop Suitability Modelling**: AI identifies optimal crops for specific regions based on soil, rainfall, and temperature patterns.

- **Erosion and Degradation Mapping**: AI tracks soil erosion and degradation, informing soil restoration and anti-desertification programmes.

- **Agroforestry Planning**: AI helps integrate tree planting into farmland design, enhancing biodiversity and productivity.

These applications balance ecological health with food production and livelihoods.

3. Urbanisation and Land Use Change.

AI aids in managing the impact of urban development on ecosystems:

- **Urban Expansion Modelling**: AI predicts patterns of urban growth, guiding zoning policies that preserve green spaces.

- **Ecological Corridor Planning**: AI supports the design of wildlife corridors that connect fragmented habitats.

- **Land Use Change Detection**: AI detects shifts from natural landscapes to human-made environments, prompting rapid policy responses.

These tools protect critical ecosystems amid expanding development.

Ecosystem Restoration and
Climate Resilience

1. Restoration Site Selection and Monitoring

AI enhances reforestation and ecosystem recovery efforts:

- **Degraded Land Mapping**: AI identifies degraded or desertified land suitable for reforestation or soil rehabilitation.

- **Species Recommendation**: AI suggests native plant species suitable for local conditions and climate adaptation.

- **Progress Monitoring**: AI tracks vegetation regrowth, biodiversity return, and soil health over time using remote sensing.

This enables cost-effective and ecologically sound restoration programmes.

2. Climate Adaptation and Biodiversity Resilience

AI supports strategies that prepare ecosystems for climate change:

- **Habitat Connectivity Models**: AI maps pathways for species migration in response to climate shifts, supporting resilient landscapes.

- **Biodiversity Risk Forecasting**: AI anticipates species or ecosystem vulnerabilities, allowing proactive protection measures.

- **Green Infrastructure Planning**: AI recommends nature-based solutions, such as wetlands or tree belts, to buffer climate impacts.

These interventions increase ecosystem resilience while benefiting human communities.

Ethical and Practical Considerations

AI for terrestrial conservation must be implemented responsibly:

- **Community Participation**: Indigenous and local communities must be engaged and benefit from AI applications in land and biodiversity management.

- **Data Justice**: Data collected from natural areas must be governed transparently, respecting sovereignty and ethical standards.

- **Inclusivity and Access**: Conservation organisations in the Global South must have access to affordable, open AI tools.

- **Environmental Cost of AI**: AI infrastructure should minimise its carbon footprint, especially when deployed in remote areas.

- **Avoiding Technosolutionism**: AI must complement—not replace—traditional knowledge, participatory approaches, and governance reform.

Embedding ethics in AI design ensures long-term sustainability and legitimacy.

Case Studies and Applications

1. Wildlife Insights (Global) A collaborative platform using AI to process millions of camera trap images, identifying species and supporting global biodiversity research.

2. Rainforest Connection (Multiple Countries) Uses AI and old smartphones placed in trees to detect logging activity in real-time by identifying chainsaw sounds.

3. Microsoft's AI for Earth (Global): Funds AI projects focused on land use, species conservation, and sustainable agriculture, particularly in biodiversity hotspots.

4. Sentinel Hub and EO Browser (Europe): These platforms provide AI-powered access to satellite imagery for land cover classification and deforestation monitoring.

5. TreesAI (UK and Kenya): Combines AI and satellite imagery to measure carbon sequestration in reforestation projects, supporting carbon credit systems.

Strategies for Scaling AI for SDG 15

1. **Strengthen Local Partnerships:** Collaborate with local NGOs, governments, and communities to ensure relevant, impactful solutions.

2. **Invest in Open-Source Tools:** Promote transparency and accessibility through open AI models, datasets, and platforms.

3. **Support Interdisciplinary Research:** Encourage collaboration between ecologists, data scientists, and social scientists.

4. **Incorporate Traditional Knowledge:** Blend AI insights with indigenous and local knowledge for holistic ecosystem management.

5. **Develop Clear Ethical Guidelines**: Establish principles for responsible data use, algorithm development, and stakeholder inclusion.

6. **Build Capacity**: Train conservation practitioners in AI literacy and ensure ongoing support for adoption and maintenance.

AI can play a pivotal role in reversing land degradation, conserving biodiversity, and building climate resilience on land.

By enhancing monitoring, enabling predictive planning, and supporting restoration, AI strengthens our collective capacity to achieve SDG 15. But its deployment must prioritise inclusion, transparency, and sustainability.

The path to restoring life on land is not purely technological it is also social and political.

When AI is harnessed as a complement to community action, policy reform, and ecological knowledge, it becomes a force for regeneration, justice, and stewardship of our planet's terrestrial ecosystems.

Chapter 19:
AI for Peace, Justice and Strong Institutions
(SDG 16)

Sustainable Development Goal 16: Peace, Justice and Strong Institutions aims to promote peaceful and inclusive societies, provide access to justice for all, and build effective, accountable, and transparent institutions. The goal acknowledges that sustainable development cannot thrive in the absence of law, human rights, trust in public institutions, and political stability.

Artificial Intelligence (AI) is increasingly being applied across justice systems, public governance, and peacebuilding. From improving access to legal services and detecting corruption to supporting early warning systems for conflict, AI has the potential to make institutions more efficient, equitable, and responsive.

However, its deployment also raises significant concerns around bias, surveillance, and accountability. This chapter explores the dual potential of AI to either enhance or undermine SDG 16 and presents a vision for responsible AI use to strengthen justice and governance systems.

AI for Access to Justice

1. Legal Information and Assistance

AI tools can democratise legal knowledge and help people understand and navigate legal systems:

- **Legal Chatbots:** AI-powered chatbots offer real-time responses to common legal queries in accessible language.

- **Document Analysis:** AI helps users analyse contracts or legal notices, identifying risks or missing information.

- **Legal Aid Platforms:** AI connects individuals with appropriate legal aid services based on case type, urgency, and location.

These tools expand access to legal services, especially in regions with lawyer shortages or linguistic barriers.

2. Case Management and Court Efficiency

AI improves the functioning of judicial systems:

- **Case Prioritisation:** AI helps courts manage caseloads by identifying urgent or complex cases.

- **Judgment Prediction**: Some systems use AI to forecast legal outcomes based on historical rulings, informing legal strategy.

- **Document Automation**: AI generates standard legal documents, reducing clerical burdens.

By easing backlogs and streamlining procedures, AI enhances the delivery of timely justice.

3. Transparency and Legal Accountability
AI can shine a light on judicial decisions and improve trust in legal systems:

- **Open Judgement Databases**: Natural Language Processing (NLP) organises and summarises large collections of court rulings.

- **Bias Detection**: AI audits case outcomes to detect patterns of racial, gender, or socioeconomic bias.

- **Public Legal Education**: AI curates' legal content for civic education, empowering citizens to know their rights.

Such tools foster more accountable and equitable legal systems.

AI in Governance and Public Administration

1. Enhancing Government Services

AI helps governments deliver services more efficiently and responsively:

- **Smart Complaint Systems:** AI triages citizen grievances and routes them to relevant departments.

- **Service Delivery Optimisation:** AI predicts demand for health, education, or housing services, guiding resource allocation.

- **Digital Identity Verification:** AI facilitates secure, inclusive digital ID systems for accessing public services.

These applications can improve citizen satisfaction and reduce bureaucracy.

2. Fighting Corruption and Ensuring Accountability

AI supports transparency and integrity in governance:

- **Procurement Oversight:** AI detects anomalies in tendering processes, flagging potential fraud.

- **Budget Analysis:** Machine learning identifies misallocated funds or unusual spending patterns.

- **Whistleblower Protection:** AI enables secure, anonymous reporting platforms that safeguard sources.

These tools reinforce institutional integrity and public trust.

3. Civic Engagement and Democratic Participation
AI fosters greater participation in public decision-making:

- **Sentiment Analysis:** AI monitors social media and surveys to assess public opinion on policies.

- **Deliberative Platforms:** AI summarises citizen input in participatory budgeting or town hall meetings.

- **Voting Access and Security:** AI enhances biometric systems, electoral roll management, and voting system monitoring.

With inclusive design, these tools strengthen democratic governance.

AI for Peacebuilding and Conflict Prevention

1. Early Warning and Conflict Prediction

AI supports timely responses to potential crises:

- **Conflict Modelling:** AI analyses social, political, and economic indicators to forecast conflict risks.

- **Social Media Monitoring:** AI tracks hate speech, misinformation, or incitement to violence.

- **Humanitarian Response Planning:** AI simulates displacement and infrastructure damage from conflict scenarios.

These systems inform pre-emptive action by governments and international organisations.

2. Post-Conflict Recovery and Transitional Justice

AI supports reconstruction and justice in post-conflict societies:

- **War Crimes Documentation:** AI analyses video and satellite evidence of human rights violations.

- **Missing Persons Identification:** AI matches biometric and DNA data to reunite families.

- **Transitional Justice Support**: AI helps analyse testimonies, victim records, and legal archives.

These applications aid in truth-seeking, accountability, and healing.

3. Dialogue and Reconciliation Platforms
AI can support inclusive and safe dialogue:

- **Translation and Moderation**: AI enables multilingual, moderated online forums for community dialogue.

- **Bias Mitigation in Content**: AI filters hate speech and misinformation from public discourse.

- **Conflict Simulation Games**: AI-driven simulations help youth explore peacebuilding scenarios and empathy building.

When carefully designed, these tools promote social cohesion and conflict transformation.

Ethical and Governance Challenges

Deploying AI for justice and governance involves serious risks:

- **Bias and Discrimination**: AI can perpetuate systemic biases if trained on unrepresentative or prejudiced data.

- **Lack of Transparency**: Opaque algorithms undermine public accountability and legal due process.

- **Surveillance and Privacy Violations**: AI can be misused to monitor dissent or marginalised communities.

- **Power Imbalances**: Without safeguards, AI can centralise control in governments or corporations.

- **Access and Inclusion**: Marginalised communities may lack access to AI-enhanced services or protections.

These risks necessitate robust governance, regulation, and civil oversight.

Case Studies and Applications

1. **Case Law Analytics (France):** Provides legal professionals with AI-based predictions and risk assessments based on past court rulings.

2. UN Global Pulse (International): Uses AI to analyse public sentiment and early warning indicators for humanitarian and peacebuilding efforts.

3. HURUmap (Africa): Uses AI to make public data on governance and elections accessible through maps and visual tools.

4. Estonia's e-Government Services: Integrates AI into digital identity systems, citizen services, and policy design.

5. The Hague Declaration on Responsible AI: A global initiative promoting ethical principles in the use of AI for legal and justice systems.

Strategies for Scaling AI for SDG 16

1. **Establish Ethical AI Frameworks**: Legal and ethical standards should govern the design and use of AI in public institutions.

2. **Promote Algorithmic Transparency**: AI tools used in governance must be explainable and open to audit.

3. **Ensure Civic Participation**: Civil society must have a voice in AI policy, design, and oversight.

4. **Invest in Open Legal Data:** Accessible, anonymised court and government records support equitable AI development.

5. **Build Institutional Capacity:** Public servants, judges, and legal professionals need AI literacy and training.

6. **Safeguard Human Rights:** Strong data protection laws and human rights impact assessments must accompany AI deployment.

AI holds the potential to make governance more transparent, legal systems more accessible, and societies more peaceful. Yet these outcomes are not guaranteed. The deployment of AI for SDG 16 must be guided by values of justice, inclusion, and accountability.

To ensure that AI strengthens rather than undermines democratic institutions, it must be developed and governed in partnership with affected communities, civil society, and public institutions. Only then can AI truly become a tool for peace, justice, and strong institutions.

Chapter 20:
AI for Partnerships for the Goals
(SDG 17)

Sustainable Development Goal 17: Partnerships for the Goals underscores the importance of revitalising global cooperation for sustainable development. It highlights the need for effective public-private partnerships, technology transfer, capacity building, policy coherence, and inclusive multilateralism. Achieving the other 16 SDGs hinges upon robust collaborations across borders and sectors.

Artificial Intelligence (AI), as a cross-cutting and rapidly evolving technology, offers both the challenge and opportunity of transforming global development efforts.

Its successful integration into SDG strategies depends on building inclusive, ethical, and collaborative systems that benefit all stakeholders. This chapter explores how AI can facilitate partnerships, enhance global capacity, promote data sharing, and support effective governance and financing for sustainable development.

Enabling Multistakeholder Collaboration through AI

1. Strengthening Public-Private Partnerships

AI fosters collaboration between governments, businesses, and civil society:

- **Data-Driven Decision Making**: AI systems provide real-time insights to policymakers and private sector actors, enabling coordinated action.

- **Collaborative Platforms**: AI-powered tools support joint planning, impact tracking, and resource sharing across institutions.

- **Innovation Hubs**: Governments and private companies co-develop AI research and infrastructure through technology incubators and challenge funds.

These initiatives amplify the reach and efficiency of sustainable development interventions.

2. Facilitating International Cooperation

AI helps bridge global divides by enabling shared knowledge and solutions:

- **Multilingual Communication:** AI-powered translation tools support dialogue across languages and cultures in international forums.

- **Virtual Collaboration:** AI optimises remote coordination, scheduling, and project management, making international partnerships more efficient.

- **Global Challenge Mapping:** AI analyses international datasets to identify shared development challenges and align collaborative efforts.

Through these tools, AI enables more agile, inclusive international engagement.

Advancing Capacity Building and Knowledge Sharing

1. Democratising AI Education and Skills

AI can empower institutions and individuals in developing countries:

- **AI-Enabled Education Platforms:** Personalised learning tools help learners build technical and analytical skills.

- **Open Curriculum Initiatives:** Global universities and companies collaborate on open-access AI training materials.

- **AI Fellowships and Exchange Programmes:** Cross-border training opportunities promote knowledge transfer and local expertise development.

Investing in human capacity is critical for sustainable and inclusive AI adoption.

2. Supporting South-South and Triangular Cooperation: AI enhances the effectiveness of South-South development partnerships:

- **Contextual Solutions:** AI models developed in the Global South reflect local priorities and constraints.

- **Peer Learning Platforms:** AI curates and recommends case studies of successful development interventions between countries.

- **Regional AI Centres:** Shared research and development facilities foster local ownership and innovation.

Such approaches challenge North-South technology dependencies and promote sovereignty.

3. Building Institutional Readiness
To integrate AI, institutions must be equipped with necessary infrastructure and governance:

- **Digital Transformation Roadmaps**: AI helps assess organisational readiness and identify capacity gaps.

- **Public Sector AI Guidelines**: AI supports the creation of ethical, legal, and technical frameworks for government adoption.

- **Risk Management Tools**: AI models assist institutions in identifying data, cyber, or policy risks associated with digital adoption.

Robust institutions are foundational to sustainable and scalable AI deployment.

Promoting Data Sharing and Digital Infrastructure

1. Interoperability and Open Standards
AI thrives on connected, high-quality data:

- **Data Harmonisation Tools:** AI helps align data from different formats, systems, and sectors.

- **Metadata Generation:** NLP-based tools create standardised descriptions of datasets for easier sharing.

- **Open Data Ecosystems:** Governments and partners publish development data using AI-curated platforms that enhance usability.

These strategies facilitate global problem-solving and innovation.

2. Improving Global Digital Infrastructure
AI supports the development of resilient digital systems:

- **Infrastructure Mapping:** AI identifies gaps in internet connectivity and digital services, informing infrastructure investment.

- **Predictive Maintenance:** AI monitors and maintains data centres and communication networks, reducing downtime.

- **Sustainable Computing:** AI optimises energy use in cloud infrastructure, reducing carbon emissions.

Equitable access to digital infrastructure underpins inclusive AI deployment.

3. Ensuring Data Justice and Sovereignty

AI governance must uphold fairness and rights:

- **Privacy-Preserving Technologies**: AI systems use federated learning or differential privacy to protect sensitive information.

- **Inclusive Data Governance Models**: Community-led data initiatives ensure consent and participation in data use.

- **Sovereign Data Strategies**: Nations design AI policies that protect local control over critical datasets.

Respecting data rights builds trust and legitimacy in digital partnerships.

Mobilising Finance and Scaling Innovation

1. AI for Development Finance and Impact Investing

AI unlocks new models of sustainable investment:

- **Project Scoring**: AI analyses risk and impact to prioritise funding for high-impact SDG initiatives.

- **Monitoring and Evaluation (M&E):** AI tracks outcomes in real time, reducing reporting burdens and increasing accountability.

- **Fraud Detection:** AI enhances due diligence and financial oversight for donors and lenders.

This boosts donor confidence and accelerates impact-driven funding.

2. Scaling Social Innovation Ecosystems

AI supports the growth of inclusive and mission-driven ventures:

- **Matchmaking Platforms:** AI connects social entrepreneurs with funders, mentors, and collaborators.

- **Ecosystem Mapping:** AI visualises innovation networks, revealing gaps and synergies.

- **Impact Forecasting:** AI predicts the scalability and societal benefits of start-up models.

These capabilities help incubators and accelerators optimise support for innovators.

3. Digital Public Goods and Shared Infrastructure

Partnerships can build AI tools as digital public goods:

- **Open-Source Algorithms:** Governments and developers collaborate on foundational models for common challenges (e.g. health diagnostics, agricultural prediction).

- **Shared Cloud Platforms:** Global AI infrastructure can be built on pooled investments for developing regions.

- **Common Governance Protocols:** International partnerships create norms for responsible AI sharing and reuse.

Collective stewardship of AI tools promotes inclusive, sustainable innovation.

Ethical Considerations and Inclusive Governance

As AI is embedded in global development partnerships, ethical governance is essential:

- **Avoiding Technological Imperialism:** Partnerships must not impose external AI models without local adaptation.

- **Ensuring Representation:** Marginalised voices must shape the design and use of AI in global development.

- **Mitigating Power Asymmetries:** Collaborative models should avoid concentrating influence in major tech firms or donor nations.

- **Supporting Local Ownership:** AI capacity should be built locally to ensure sustainability and cultural fit.

- **Upholding Transparency and Accountability:** All AI systems used in partnerships must be open to review and evaluation. Ethics must be embedded at every level—from code to policy.

Case Studies and Applications

1. AI4D Africa (Pan-African) A partnership between IDRC, GIZ, and African universities to build AI research networks, support start-ups, and strengthen capacity on the continent.

2. UNDP and Pulse Lab Jakarta (Indonesia) Uses AI to analyse citizen feedback and social media for development planning, with open-source tools co-created with local stakeholders.

3. The GovStack Initiative (Global) Brings together governments and tech partners to co-develop reusable digital building blocks for public service delivery.

4. Open AI for the SDGs (Global) A collaboration among tech companies, NGOs, and UN bodies to build open-source AI tools for environmental and humanitarian goals.

5. Data Science for Social Good (Global) A fellowship programme matching data scientists with social sector organisations to solve development problems using AI.

Strategies for Scaling AI for SDG 17

1. **Foster Inclusive AI Governance:** Develop multilateral frameworks that balance innovation with ethics and equity.

2. **Invest in AI Infrastructure for Development:** Prioritise connectivity, cloud, and compute infrastructure in development finance.

3. **Support South-Led Innovation:** Fund and showcase AI projects led by researchers and institutions in the Global South.

4. **Promote Responsible Tech Transfer:** Ensure that AI tools and knowledge are shared with safeguards and contextual support.

5. **Cultivate Global AI Literacy:** Expand training opportunities in AI for development practitioners, policymakers, and civil society.

6. **Measure Impact Transparently:** Use AI to track SDG progress but validate results with community engagement and participatory methods.

AI can play a critical role in strengthening the partnerships, infrastructure, and innovation ecosystems needed to accelerate the SDGs. It offers a means to unlock insights, foster inclusive collaboration, and mobilise resources for impact. However, the promise of AI will only be realised through ethical governance, equitable access, and genuine global cooperation.

To achieve SDG 17, we must view AI not merely as a tool but as a space for partnership—an opportunity to reimagine how humanity collaborates for sustainable progress. Through shared purpose and collective stewardship, AI can become a foundation for a more connected, fair, and sustainable world.

Chapter 21:
Integrated AI Strategies for Accelerating the SDGs

As the global community races to meet the 2030 Sustainable Development Goals (SDGs), the challenge is no longer just about identifying which tools to use, but about integrating them in cohesive, efficient, and ethical strategies. Artificial Intelligence (AI), with its vast applications across sectors, offers a transformative capability.

However, for AI to contribute effectively, it must be integrated into development strategies in a way that aligns with human values, cross-sector collaboration, and inclusive governance. This chapter presents a blueprint for integrated AI strategies that accelerate the implementation of all SDGs holistically, beyond individual targets or sectors.

Why Integration Matters

Sustainable development challenges are interlinked. Poverty reduction influences health outcomes; education impacts gender equality and economic growth; climate action intersects with life on land and water. Similarly, AI's influence is cross-cutting—making integration a natural and necessary approach:

- **Efficiency Gains:** Integrated strategies allow AI applications to support multiple goals simultaneously, e.g., predictive analytics for agriculture also supports hunger, climate, and economic goals.

- **Policy Coherence:** AI enables consistent and data-driven policy evaluation, ensuring different departments and stakeholders are aligned.

- **Avoiding Silos:** Without integration, AI solutions risk duplication, fragmentation, and contradictory impacts.

AI must be treated not as an isolated tool, but as a connective enabler across SDGs.

Frameworks for Integrated AI Deployment

1. Cross-Sectoral AI Innovation Platforms

Governments and institutions should create shared platforms for AI experimentation and deployment that cut across departments and domains:

- **Innovation Sandboxes:** Regulated environments for testing AI solutions involving multiple ministries (e.g., environment, health, economy).

- **Unified Data Lakes**: AI systems trained on interoperable data from education, health, transport, and agriculture for richer insights.

- **Joint Research Centres**: Universities and think tanks collaborate on multidisciplinary AI projects for SDG solutions.

Such platforms accelerate policy experimentation and the scale-up of AI for social good.

2. SDG-Aligned AI Development Guidelines

To guide integration, countries and institutions should adopt clear guidelines:

- **AI-SDG Compatibility Matrix**: Mapping AI use cases against their impact on each SDG target.

- **Risk-Benefit Assessments**: Evaluating unintended consequences and ensuring ethical safeguards.

- **Inclusion Protocols**: Ensuring diverse representation in AI design and deployment processes.

These frameworks ensure AI contributes to the SDGs as a whole, not just selectively.

Use Cases for Integrated AI Strategies

1. Urban Planning for Sustainable Cities
AI can be applied to integrated city management by:

- Mapping transportation patterns, emissions, housing needs, and health outcomes to design equitable and green cities (SDGs 3, 11, 13).
- Forecasting infrastructure strain based on projected population growth and climate data.
- Optimising urban agriculture and food distribution to improve food security.

2. AI in Crisis Response and Resilience
AI can predict, detect, and coordinate responses to crises:
- Early warning systems using AI for disease outbreaks, natural disasters, or conflict.
- Cross-sector coordination tools for humanitarian logistics, public health, and food distribution.
- Real-time feedback tools to track and adapt policies during crises.

This supports SDGs 2, 3, 6, 13, and 16 simultaneously.

3. Integrated Education and Employment Systems
AI can support lifelong learning pathways aligned with labour market trends:

- Identifying skills gaps across regions and populations.
- Customising learning content and career guidance.
- Matching educational outcomes with sustainable economic sectors.

This bridges SDGs 4, 8, 9, and 10.

4. Environmental Monitoring for Planetary Boundaries

AI enables coordinated action across ecosystems:

- Monitoring land, air, and water health simultaneously.
- Predicting cumulative environmental impacts of policies.
- Coordinating biodiversity conservation with carbon mitigation and food production.

These systems address SDGs 6, 13, 14, and 15 in an integrated manner.

Governance and Policy Mechanisms

1. Whole-of-Government Approaches

National digital transformation strategies must position AI as a shared resource:

- **Chief AI Officers or Digital Envoys** coordinate AI deployment across ministries.
- **Inter-ministerial AI Councils** ensure policy coherence and accountability.
- **AI-SDG Implementation Units** track alignment with national SDG targets.

2. Participatory AI Policymaking.

- **Citizen Assemblies on AI** gather public input on priorities and ethics.
- **Digital Inclusion Forums** involve marginalised groups in AI deployment decisions.

- **Multi-stakeholder AI Observatories** monitor the impact of AI across SDGs.

Inclusive governance is crucial for legitimacy and effectiveness.

3. AI-Driven SDG Monitoring and Reporting:

- AI can analyse and visualise real-time SDG progress indicators.
- Natural language processing automates SDG report generation from diverse sources.
- Predictive models simulate SDG scenarios and trade-offs.

This enables more responsive and adaptive policy cycles.

Challenges in Integrating AI for the SDGs

- **Technical Fragmentation:** Lack of interoperability and standardisation limits integration.

- **Data Silos:** Inaccessible or incompatible data across sectors hinders AI's cross-cutting capabilities.

- **Funding Gaps:** Most AI investment is private and profit-driven, misaligned with SDG needs.

- **Digital Inequality:** Countries and communities lacking digital infrastructure cannot benefit equally.

- **Ethical Blind Spots:** Without integration, AI may optimise one goal while undermining others (e.g., surveillance for security undermining human rights).

Enablers of Success

1. **Interoperable AI Infrastructure:** Invest in platforms and protocols that allow cross-sector AI integration.

2. **Sustainable AI Funding Models:** Public and philanthropic financing for open-source, SDG-aligned AI solutions.

3. **Capacity Building Across Sectors:** Train policymakers, civil servants, and community leaders in AI-SDG integration.

4. **Global Cooperation:** International bodies must support AI integration through guidelines, funding, and shared infrastructure.

5. **AI for SDG Labs:** Incubators that pilot and scale integrated AI use cases in real-world contexts.

The greatest power of AI for sustainable development lies not in isolated applications, but in its ability to connect systems, break silos, and accelerate collective progress. As we move toward 2030, integrated AI strategies can serve as catalysts for systems change, helping to coordinate, amplify, and accelerate our efforts across all 17 Goals.

This chapter calls on policymakers, technologists, civil society, and international organisations to think systemically about AI—not merely as a set of tools but as a connective tissue for global development. When deployed responsibly and collaboratively, AI becomes more than innovation; it becomes the infrastructure of transformation.

Chapter 22:
The Future of AI and Sustainable Development.

Opportunities and Risks

As we approach the midpoint of the 2030 Agenda, the conversation about the role of Artificial Intelligence (AI) in achieving the Sustainable Development Goals (SDGs) is shifting from 'if' to 'how'. AI is becoming ubiquitous—from smartphones to health diagnostics to national development strategies. Its integration into sustainable development is no longer speculative; it is underway. Yet with this momentum comes a dual imperative: to harness AI's vast potential while proactively managing its risks.

This chapter offers a forward-looking analysis of the future landscape of AI in global development, exploring both the transformative opportunities it presents and the emerging risks it may pose.

Emerging Opportunities for AI in Sustainable Development.

1. Precision Policy and Governance
AI will increasingly empower governments to formulate, test, and adapt policies in real-time:

- **Policy Simulation:** AI can model the likely outcomes of policy choices, allowing decision-makers to assess trade-offs and design optimal interventions.

- **Predictive Governance:** Forecasting tools will help predict social, economic, and environmental trends to inform proactive governance.

- **Responsive Public Services:** AI will enable real-time service delivery tailored to citizen needs, reducing waste and improving impact.

2. Personalised Education, Healthcare, and Social Support

AI's capacity for personalisation will improve outcomes across social services:

- **Adaptive Learning:** AI-driven education platforms will evolve based on learner behaviour, preferences, and needs.

- **Precision Medicine:** AI will enable individualised treatment plans based on genetics, lifestyle, and medical history.

- **Targeted Social Protection:** AI will identify vulnerable populations and match them with tailored support packages.

3. Decentralised and Citizen-Led Innovation

The future of AI is not confined to labs and corporations:

- **AI-as-a-Service**: Open-source platforms and low-code/no-code tools will democratise AI development.

- **Community Innovation**: Grassroots groups and civic technologists will build AI tools for local issues, from climate resilience to access to justice.

- **Participatory AI Design**: Citizens will co-create algorithms that reflect local needs, values, and languages.

4. Climate Adaptation and Environmental Stewardship

AI's role in environmental sustainability will deepen:

- **Planetary Modelling**: AI will help simulate and monitor complex planetary systems, aiding in ecosystem and climate management.

- **Resource Efficiency**: Smart grids, sustainable agriculture, and circular economy systems will increasingly rely on AI for optimisation.

- **Environmental Justice:** AI will be used to monitor and predict pollution and environmental degradation in marginalised communities.

5. Global Cooperation and Digital Diplomacy
AI will shape the institutions and norms of international development:

- **Shared Platforms for SDG Monitoring:** Global datasets and AI tools will support collective action and mutual accountability.

- **AI Diplomacy:** Countries will collaborate on AI standards, safety, and ethics, framing AI as a public good.

- **Global AI Commons:** Institutions may steward open AI models and infrastructure for equitable use.

Risks and Challenges on the Horizon

1. Deepening Inequality
Without careful intervention, AI may exacerbate global disparities:

- **Digital Divides:** Unequal access to AI infrastructure, skills, and investment may reinforce the marginalisation of poorer countries.

- **Data Colonialism:** Data extraction from the Global South to power AI systems in the Global North risks new forms of exploitation.

- **Monopolisation:** The dominance of a few companies in AI innovation may limit the agency of smaller players and countries.

2. Algorithmic Harm and Ethical Failures

As AI becomes embedded in governance and society, ethical lapses can have systemic impacts:

- **Bias and Discrimination:** AI models trained on skewed data can perpetuate or intensify inequality.

- **Opacity and Accountability:** Black-box algorithms hinder transparency, complicating legal and ethical oversight.

- **Autonomy Erosion:** As AI makes more decisions, concerns arise around individual agency, consent, and responsibility.

3. Environmental Impact of AI Itself

Ironically, AI can contribute to environmental degradation:

- **Energy Consumption:** Large-scale AI training models require immense computational resources, often powered by fossil fuels.

- **E-waste:** AI's integration in devices accelerates electronic waste generation.

- **Sustainable Design Gaps:** Many AI tools are not optimised for energy or material efficiency.

4. Surveillance and Repression

AI technologies can be used to undermine peace, rights, and democratic values:

- **State Surveillance:** Governments may deploy facial recognition and predictive policing to control populations.

- **Authoritarian AI:** Illiberal regimes may use AI to suppress dissent, manipulate information, and entrench power.

- **Corporate Surveillance Capitalism:** Data collection for profit may erode privacy and skew civic discourse.

5. Governance Lag

Policy frameworks often lag behind technological change:

- **Regulatory Gaps**: Many countries lack AI-specific legislation or ethical guidelines.

- **Global Norm Deficits**: There is no universal agreement on the rights, responsibilities, and red lines of AI use.

- **Institutional Readiness**: Public institutions may lack the skills, capacity, or agility to govern AI effectively.

Recommendations for Future AI-Driven Development

1. Adopt Holistic AI Governance Models:

- **Principle-Based Regulation**: Establish flexible but firm rules rooted in human rights, sustainability, and inclusion.
- **Multistakeholder Councils**: Involve civil society, academia, and the private sector in AI oversight.
- **Dynamic Policy Frameworks**: Use AI itself to support adaptive policymaking that evolves with technological change.

2. Invest in Local and Inclusive AI Ecosystems:

- **Support Local Innovation**: Fund grassroots AI initiatives that reflect local realities.

- **AI Literacy for All:** Mainstream AI education in schools, universities, and public administration.
- **Bridge the Infrastructure Gap:** Prioritise investments in connectivity, hardware, and skills in under-resourced areas.

3. Embed Sustainability in AI Design

- **Green AI Standards:** Mandate energy efficiency and environmental reporting for large AI models.
- **Circular Economy Integration:** Design AI systems for recyclability, repairability, and long-term use.
- **Environmental Impact Audits:** Require life cycle assessments for AI infrastructure.

4. Build an AI Commons for the SDGs

- **Open Data and Models:** Share AI tools that support SDG implementation freely and equitably.
- **International Funding Mechanisms:** Create a global fund for AI for Good projects, prioritising low-income contexts.
- **Public-Interest Algorithms:** Develop AI for health, education, and climate as non-proprietary, interoperable tools.

5. Reimagine Development Leadership for the AI Age

- **Ethical Leadership:** Equip leaders with both technical understanding and moral courage.
- **Youth Inclusion:** Integrate youth voices and innovation into AI governance and development strategy.
- **South-South Cooperation:** Encourage AI collaboration among developing countries to build solidarity and shared capacity.

The future of AI and sustainable development is not predetermined. It will be shaped by our choices—by what we prioritise, how we design and govern technology, and who gets to participate in its creation and use.

If we take the path of equity, collaboration, and foresight, AI can be one of the most powerful accelerators of human and planetary progress ever created.

But if we fail to address its risks and imbalances, AI may entrench the very inequalities and crises the SDGs aim to overcome.

This chapter calls for a long-term, values-based vision for AI in development: one rooted in justice, solidarity, and stewardship. The future remains unwritten, and AI is a pen. It is up to us what kind of world we write with it.

Chapter 23:
A Call to Action for Ethical and Inclusive AI for Global Good

As we conclude this journey across the *17 Sustainable Development Goals (SDGs)* and the transformative power of Artificial Intelligence (AI), one truth stands clear: AI is not a distant future it is a present force.

The decisions we make now will shape whether AI accelerates inclusive, sustainable development or amplifies inequality and environmental harm.

This chapter brings together the insights from across the book to frame a shared call to action for all stakeholders—from governments and innovators to communities and individuals who must lead, regulate, and shape AI for global good.

The Crossroads of Promise and Peril

AI presents a historic opportunity to reimagine human progress. It can improve lives, expand capabilities, and help us achieve what once seemed impossible.
But this power comes with profound responsibility:

- **Promise**: From eradicating poverty to enabling climate resilience, AI can target inefficiencies, predict future needs, and personalise services.

- **Peril**: AI can reinforce bias, undermine privacy, centralise control, and accelerate environmental destruction if left unchecked.

The direction we take depends on whether we anchor AI in principles of equity, transparency, sustainability, and collaboration.

A Summary of What We've Learned

1. **AI is already accelerating the SDGs**: Across every SDG, we see AI applications—from predictive analytics in agriculture to smart grids in energy, and from digital learning tools to AI-supported disease diagnostics.

2. **Integration is critical**: The power of AI is magnified when it bridges silos and drives systems-level change. Integrated strategies are more efficient, equitable, and scalable.

3. **Ethical governance must lead innovation**: The velocity of AI development must not outpace our ability to govern it. Clear, adaptive, and inclusive ethical frameworks are needed at every level.

4. **Inclusion and representation matter:** Marginalised communities must help shape AI solutions, not merely receive them. This includes data ownership, co-design, and capacity building.

5. **AI's environmental footprint must be addressed:** Green AI energy-efficient, transparent, and circular is essential to avoid undermining sustainability goals.

6. **Global cooperation is non-negotiable:** No country can succeed alone in governing or leveraging AI. Global norms, shared infrastructure, and collaborative innovation are key.

A Call to Action for Stakeholders

For Policymakers:
- **Develop national AI strategies** aligned with the SDGs, rooted in ethics, inclusion, and long-term vision.
- **Invest in AI capacity building**, from schools to public institutions.
- **Adopt smart regulation** that enables innovation while protecting rights and ecosystems.
- **Support open data and digital public goods** for equitable AI access.

For the Private Sector:
- **Embed ethical AI practices** into design, development, and deployment.
- **Invest in responsible innovation,** especially in underrepresented regions and sectors.
- **Partner with governments and civil society** to align AI products with development goals.
- **Report transparently** on AI impacts, risks, and mitigation measures.

For Academia and Researchers
- **Prioritise interdisciplinary research** that connects technical AI with social, ethical, and environmental dimensions.
- **Open-source findings and tools** to maximise their reach and impact.
- **Work with communities** to ensure research reflects real world needs.
- **Train the next generation** of AI developers as ethical, inclusive, and globally minded innovators.

For Civil Society:
- **Hold AI systems accountable,** especially where they affect human rights, livelihoods, or the environment.
- **Educate communities** about AI, rights, and digital participation.

- **Co-create solutions** with local knowledge and lived experience.
- **Champion marginalised voices** in national and international AI dialogues.

For International Organisations:
- **Facilitate global governance frameworks** for AI that reflect diverse realities.
- **Fund open AI infrastructure** and South-led innovation.
- **Coordinate SDG data ecosystems** with AI-powered tools for real-time monitoring.
- **Bridge diplomacy and technology,** ensuring AI supports peace, not power imbalances.

Principles for the Road Ahead:
1. **Human-Centred:** Technology must serve people, not the other way around.
2. **Inclusive:** No one should be left behind in the AI transformation.
3. **Transparent:** Openness builds trust and enables better decisions.
4. **Ethical:** Equity, justice, and sustainability must guide every AI choice.
5. **Collaborative:** Partnerships are more powerful than competition in building the future we need.

AI will not solve the world's problems on its own. But used wisely, it can help us solve them faster, more precisely, and more inclusively than ever before. Whether we harness that power for good or allow it to deepen injustice will depend on our collective actions now.

This book has aimed to inspire, guide, and equip you—the reader, changemaker, or policymaker to engage with AI as a tool for global good. The work ahead will require courage, creativity, and compassion.

But most of all, it will require collaboration.

The age of AI for global good has begun.
Let us shape it, together.